THE SECRET TO
FINDING FINANCIAL FREEDOM
THROUGH FAITH AND THE
LAW OF ATTRACTION

THE SECRET TO
FINDING FINANCIAL FREEDOM
THROUGH FAITH AND THE
LAW OF ATTRACTION

Derek L Kilpatrick

authorHOUSE®

AuthorHouse™
1663 Liberty Drive
Bloomington, IN 47403
www.authorhouse.com
Phone: 1-800-839-8640

Published by AuthorHouse   06/28/2012

ISBN: 978-1-4772-1386-5 (sc)
ISBN: 978-1-4772-1387-2 (e)

DEDICATION

This book is lovingly dedicated to my Dad, Ian Kilpatrick

(1930-2000)

Your practical advice and training

concerning money management principles

has contributed greatly

to my enviable position in life of enjoying

the rich rewards of financial freedom.

Thank you, Dad.

TABLE OF CONTENTS

INTRODUCTION

Are you sick and tired of struggling financially month after month? Are you comfortable but deep down longing for that breakthrough which will lift you into another level of living? Are you looking for a new idea or insight that you just *know* on a subconscious level exists and awaits your discovery, and when you find it, it will open up the way for you to reach the place in life you know that you belong? **I think you'll be shocked by what you are about to read.** The knowledge you are looking for, right now is within your reach. One small piece of knowledge often spells the difference between failure and success. True freedom is the *result* of knowledge. The ancient text says, "You shall know the truth, and the truth shall set you free."

The cost to learn is much less of a price to pay than the price of suffering through ignorance. This book is not for everyone. Some people are quite happy being miserable, weak, sick and broke, and they have absolutely no intentions of changing, not for you, me or anyone else. But there are others like yourself who have reached the point in life where they are ready and willing to hear the instruction that will *turn* their weakness into strength, their misery into happiness, their sickness into vibrant health and their lack of money into **abundance of money**.

I am convinced that you would not even be looking on the inside of this book, if you were *not* the kind of person who is destined for great success. Something on the inside of you is telling you that there is *more* than where you are currently at in life. If you will simply listen to and follow that inward leading it will take you places beyond your fondest dreams. The good news is that many of the answers we are looking for have already been discovered, and what has worked successfully in the lives of millions of others, will work successfully in our lives also. At last *your* time has come to make the greatest discovery and break free from the torment of financial hardship and enter into **the wonderful world of financial freedom**.

This is a book of universal, unchanging and timeless principles that have been tested and proven with outstanding success by countless men and women throughout the ages. The sooner you learn and apply these principles, the sooner you will begin to see and feel positive changes in your level of happiness, health and wealth. **Right at your fingertips** are the **financial solutions** you've been waiting for that can **change your future** from being one of financial struggle to that of financial freedom.

I am talking to the *winner* on the inside of you, and I am inviting you to take this adventure with me through the pages ahead where secrets and strategies will awaken the sleeping giant within you, and will empower you with all the tools you need to make your life into the masterpiece it's supposed to be. Leap into the chapters ahead where you will be equipped to shake off the mentality that's producing your financial struggles and develop winning the mind-set that will burst open the floodgates of abundance and unleash the **total life prosperity** that you have been destined to enjoy.

It's your turn!

CHAPTER 1

THE GREATEST DISCOVERY

"The greatest revolution of our generation is the
discovery that human beings, by changing the inner attitudes
of their minds can change the outer aspects of their lives."
—William James—

Is there really a secret, a master key, a great discovery or whatever
you want to call it, which only a few privileged people know and use
to overcome life's challenges while creating an enviable life that is rich
in every way? I personally believe that there is. **Small keys can unlock
big doors**. Whatever it costs you in time and money to obtain and read
this book will be a great investment into your life. I believe that the
fresh insights that you will gain and the results they will produce, will
by far outweigh what it will cost you to receive them. There is a hidden
treasure within these pages that has been found and used by many who
have gone before us. Success does leave behind clues.

You hold in your hands a treasure chest that contains many nuggets of gold. Not only will you get something valuable out of this book, but hopefully this book will help to get something valuable out of you. Everything you need to succeed in life is already on the inside of you, waiting to be stirred and awakened. When you become aware of the riches that dwell within you, and learn how to tap into and use these great resources, the most wonderful thing that can happen to anyone will have happened to you.

"Perhaps the most important mental and spiritual principle ever discovered is that you become what you think about most of the time.

Your outer world is very much a mirror image of your inner world.

What is going on outside of you is a reflection of what is going on inside of you."

—Brian Tracy—

THE SECRET OF ANDREW CARNEGIE

When Napoleon Hill introduces his great book, "Think and Grow Rich," he refers to what he calls, "The Carnegie secret" which was entrusted to him by the great Scotsman Andrew Carnegie, who desired to pass onto the American people what he considered to be the most valuable and precious aspect of his great wealth, namely the philosophy by which his wealth was achieved. The author deliberately doesn't come out directly and say what this secret is, but states that the sincere student who is ready to hear it, will undoubtedly discover it within the pages. This is a simple yet profound approach as human beings tend to only be able to genuinely recognise something as valuable when they discover it for themselves.

The day I became truly aware of the influence my internal thoughts were having on my external results was the beginning of a new era for me. Over the centuries many great leaders and teachers have written and spoken about the power of the mind. In fact all the main religions although they disagree on many things are in agreement on this one principle, "**As a man thinketh in his heart, so is he**." Our minds are the control centre of our lives. Surely it is a great discovery when we realise that our inner world creates our outer world and that if we can change our thinking, we can change our lives. This master key which will unlock the doors to success and fulfilment in every area of your life is mentioned or referred to in every chapter of this book. You will find some repetition of concepts and principles. This is deliberate, as repetition is not only the most effective way of learning, but also the means by which the subconscious mind receives new programming from which it produces new results.

THE LAW OF INCREASE BY ASSOCIATION

It was Earl Nightingale who said, "If you surround your mind with greatness, some of it is going to rub off." When you rub your mind up against other great minds of great thinkers, your own mind will begin to sharpen. It is the law of increase by association. King Solomon is regarded to be the wisest and the richest man who ever lived, he said, "As iron sharpens iron, so one man sharpens another." He also said, "He who walks with wise men, will be wise." The suggestions that we expose our minds to on a regular basis will have a huge influence on the kind of mentality we develop. If we are privileged to do so, our association with wise men can be literal. If not however we certainly can spend an hour or so in the company of wise and successful individuals through their writings. Good leaders are usually also good readers. Through reading our minds can be exposed to new knowledge and fresh ideas, and one good idea can be the turning point in your struggle. A new thought can lead to a new life. Oliver Wendell Homes said, "Man's mind, once stretched by a new idea, never regains its original dimensions."

The majority of the frustration and unhappiness in our lives is the result of living far beneath our potential. The moment we begin to move in the direction of becoming our potential we start to feel better about ourselves. The purpose of all life is development and expression, everything created has the inherent desire to become all it is capable of being. Growth is a sign of good health, and a healthy life is vital and expressive.

To have more than you currently have, you've got to become more than you currently are. If you keep doing what you've always done, you'll keep getting the same kind of results. It has been said, "If you want to increase the quality and the quantity of your rewards in life, you just have to increase the quality and the quantity of your contribution." The law of compensation says that what you give out determines what will come back to you. When you increase the quality and the quantity of your contribution, there will be an increase in the quality and the quantity of your rewards.

UNDERSTANDING UNIVERSAL LAWS

Life is no respecter of persons. We live in a universe that is governed by law and order. These laws are established and work the same way for everyone, everywhere, all over the world. Understanding these laws and cooperating with them is the secret of success in life. Countless books have been written about the secrets of success and why not, we all want to enjoy our lives and so we should, in fact if anyone does not want to succeed in life, then they must have suppressed the God given inherent desire within them to increase and enjoy abundant life to the full. Why would anyone do this to themselves? More importantly, not only are they robbing and limiting themselves in life, but we all tend to pass our beliefs as well as our disbeliefs onto those around us who are influenced by us, both by the things we say and do. **Mindsets are transferable**, even from one generation to another, whether it is a positive mindset or a negative mindset.

A few years ago, I discovered "The Secret," the bestselling book and film by Rhonda Byrne. At first I was sceptical, I thought, I bet you have to read the whole way through to the end and then they finally tell you what the big secret is. But to my surprise, at the start of the very first chapter on page 4, the great secret is revealed. And the secret is the law of attraction! This universal law basically says that everything that is coming into your life, you are *attracting* into your life. And it is attracted to you because of the habitual thought patterns that are going on in your mind.

Just as there are natural laws, like the law of gravity for example, there are mental and spiritual universal laws also. If someone says that they don't believe in the law of gravity, it doesn't exclude them from the effects of this law. And if they violate it, the results could be disastrous. For example, if anyone jumps off a multi story building, assuming that they don't have a parachute, they will meet with concrete justice.

There are many established laws that govern our world. The law of cause and effect says that for every effect in our lives, there has to be a cause or series of causes. The great scientist Sir Isaac Newton discovered the laws of motion in our universe. He said that every action always has an opposite and equal reaction. In the bible we read that whatsoever a man sows that shall he also reap. All of these laws are saying to us basically the same thing. **Nothing just happens**. There really is no such thing as an accident. We may call it an accident, meaning that it wasn't done on purpose. But whatever happens, there *was* something that *caused* it to happen. Perhaps it was carelessness that caused the accident. Faulty brakes on the car in front of us, or being late for an appointment and driving too fast for the road conditions. We did not *intend* for it to happen, but whether we are aware of it or not, there was a *cause* that brought about the *effect*.

Not everyone wants to hear this. Some prefer to live by the philosophy that whatever is going to happen is going to happen, and that there is not much that we can do about it. This way of thinking violates the laws of the universe. The choices we make and the actions we take *influence* what's going to happen. If it looks like something is going to happen and isn't good, then there are things we can do to *prevent* it from happening, if we act early enough. Ignorance of laws does not exclude us from them. If a policeman pulls you over and says you were speeding, you could say that you were not aware of the speed limit in that particular area. He might be in a good mood and let you off with a warning, but there would have had to have been *something* that *caused* him to be in a good mood that day. Or he could simply choose to give you the ticket and advise you that the next time you will definitely be aware of the law that governs the road in that area. Then there is also the law of electricity. Ignorance of the fact that water and electrical items, when mixed together have the potential to instantly remove you from planet earth, regardless of your age, will not save you from their effects. As Bob Proctor says, "You may not understand electricity, and yet you enjoy the benefits of it. I don't know how it works. But I do know this, you can cook a man's dinner with electricity, and you can also cook the man."

There are laws made by men that differ from country to country and that can be changed from time to time. They can be broken and sometimes we can even get away with it. There are however also spiritual and mental laws that have *not* been made by men, these laws are of a higher order. Ignorance or violation of them does not serve us well, but understanding and respect for them gives us a great advantage in life, and can also bring to us rich rewards. Universal laws are always working, whether we are aware of them or not. Many great teachers throughout the ages have taught that the law of attraction is one of the most important laws that govern our universe.

THE FORCE FIELD OF MAGNETISM

"The law of attraction says that you are a living magnet, and that you attract into your life the people, circumstances and events that are in harmony with your dominant thoughts. When you think positive, optimistic, loving and successful thoughts, you create a force field of magnetism that attracts, like iron fillings to a magnet, the very things you are thinking about."

—Brian Tracy—

I had previously heard of the law of attraction and the power of personal magnetism from Brian Tracy's classic seminar, "The Psychology of Achievement." This information is life changing. It brings a new understanding of our personal responsibility in life, and that life is governed by laws, very accurate and precise universal laws. The truth is that you are creating your own future, so why not create it the way you want it to be by design, rather than by default arriving at a future that isn't anything like what you wanted.

"Your thoughts are creating everything you receive in your life, and always have done. This happens whether you consciously direct them or unconsciously react to your circumstances and create by default."
—Stephen H Lockie—

ARE YOU ATTRACTING OR REPELLING FINANCIAL SUCCESS?

In the financial arena it is said that some people are money magnets and others seem to be money repellents. And that if you were to equally distribute all the wealth in the world today it wouldn't be long before it would all be back in the same hands again. This is not an accident, **money goes where it is welcomed and it stays where it is respected**. Some people say that money is not important. Well if someone was to say that *you* were not important would you stay around for long? Money not only talks, but money seems to hear as well. I have never heard a wealthy person say that money isn't important, but I *have* heard plenty of broke people saying it. There is a magnetic power radiating from each one of us and *whatever* you respect you will attract, and what you disrespect you will repel.

Our thoughts and feelings about money have a huge influence on the amount of money we have in our lives. Our thoughts are on two levels, conscious and subconscious. The subconscious mind stores all the information we have received and believed throughout our lives. This internal programming has a major influence on our behaviour, and ultimately also on our experiences. If we have been programmed to think that money is the root of all evil, we will on a subconscious level repel money away from us.

To say that money is not important is ignorance and usually it is a defensive statement made by those who don't have very much of it and are trying to justify why. Anyone who has ever experienced the humiliation of poverty *knows* that money is important. If your employer told you that they will no longer be paying you from this month onward, I suspect you would be looking for another job. When the direct debits start to fail and the electricity gets cut off, when you and your family start to feel cold and hungry, you'll eventually realise that **money is important**. Let's honestly settle the issue once and for all. It is far better to have money than it is to be lacking money. The truth is that money is neither the root of all evil nor the root of all happiness, but all things being equal, most people are generally happier when they have money than they are when they lack money.

"Money is power and you ought to be reasonably ambitious to have it.

I say this because you can do more good with money than you can without it."

—Russell Conwell—

THE SPIRIT OF AMBITION

I recently visited a certain town centre in Scotland that I hadn't been near for several years. I was so surprised and saddened to see how run down it had become. All the way up the high street many shops had closed down and were boarded up, the few that remained open were mainly charity shops. A few years previously, approximately five miles from the town, a large new shopping centre had been opened. Everything was all under the one roof and with the benefit of free parking available as well, everyone was spending their money at the new facility. I am not planning on discussing the politics of out of town shopping centres here, the simple point I am making is this, the main reason for the run down look and decline of the town centre mentioned was simply that there was a lack of money coming into it.

Whether it is an individual property or a town, a city centre, or even a nation, if the people living in it have not been encouraged to have some ambition for achievement, the place is headed for decline. We should not be out to discourage, criticise and condemn those who would aspire to prosper, but rather we should be thankful for those who have some ambition within them. Wherever they are, if they do nothing else, they help to make the place look better.

> "Why should I hate the man who is smarter than I am
> and who has achieved more than I have?
> I should honour him and thank God that there are men
> of that kind."
> —E. W Kenyon—

THE ABUNDANCE MENTALITY

Some are envious of the rich and successful, as if there is only so much prosperity available and they have taken away the share of everyone else for themselves. This thinking is as ludicrous as it would be if unhappy people felt that there was only so much happiness available, and all the happy people were just greedily sucking up more than their fair share, and were leaving the rest of us to be miserable. This is a win-lose philosophy. It is the mentality that in order for someone to win, someone else has to lose. Stephen Covey taught that one of the seven habits of highly effective people is to think win-win. This is an abundance mentality. It says that there is enough for us *all* to win. It is the scarcity mentality that thinks that someone else has to lose in order for me to win. This is the competitive mind, but the creative mind believes that we can complete one another, rather than compete with one another, and this way of thinking will be far more beneficial for all of us.

The kind of environment that our children are growing up in, will affect them for better or for worse. When we are surrounded by decline and lack, there tends to be a sense of hopelessness which has its negative impact on our societies. And the results are usually similar in all declining areas, drug addiction, crime and high unemployment. If this is the kind of environment you *want* to produce, then just keep on spreading the anti-prosperity message and you will achieve it. People are not usually trying to move *into* a part of town like this, they are more likely to be trying to move *out* of it. The same principle applies for a Church or an organisation of any kind, if the people within it do not *want* to change, you'll find that eventually all the individuals with any get up and go, have all got up and gone. We *are* creating our future day by day. The future of our families, our towns, our cities and even our world is in our hands. We live in a universe of abundance and there is absolutely no need for us to live in scarcity.

> "The spiritual substance from which comes all visible wealth is never depleted.
> It is right with you all the time and responds to your faith in it and your demands on it."
> —Charles Fillmore—

There are several major influences in each of our lives, from childhood until this present moment we have been *programmed* to think in certain ways, many of these deep seated thought patterns are unsupportive to our success in life, especially our financial success. So are we destined to remain the same for the rest of our days or is there a way to delete old erroneous programming and replace it with new positive supportive information? **There certainly is**.

Authority figures in our lives have probably had the greatest influence on our beliefs. Our parents, school teachers, religious leaders and our friends, all well meaning of course, but *not* all beneficial. In most cases they could only teach us what they themselves were taught. If it's good then we should hold onto it, but if not then it has to go if we are ever going to reach our true potential and create the life of our dreams. Abraham Lincoln said, "You can't help the poor by becoming one of them."

"Any religion that claims to be concerned about people
without addressing the economic conditions that strangle
them is a dry and useless religion."
—Martin Luther King—

The Subconscious Mind

Our subconscious programming will fight against new information that contradicts the old because that's what it is designed to do. The conscious mind does the reasoning, he is the watchman at the gate, and whatever he permits to enter in will stay there unless it is challenged, removed and replaced with something else.

"Above all else, guard your heart for it determines the
course of your life."
—King Solomon—

The subconscious mind is extremely powerful. It is like fertile soil and whatever is planted in it will grow and become according to its kind. Plant thoughts of fear and worry and that which you are afraid of will come to you, plant thoughts of health, wealth and happiness until they are deeply rooted in your internal subconscious hard drive and that's what will start showing up on the screen of your life. Whatever is *impressed* on your subconscious mind will be *expressed* in your life experience.

"Any idea that is held in the mind that is either feared or revered will begin at once to clothe itself in the most convenient and appropriate physical forms available."
—Andrew Carnegie—

THE POWER OF GRATITUDE AND APPRECIATION

Being grateful for what you currently have puts you in a positive vibration and attracts more things into your life to be grateful for. The other side of the coin is that complaining about what you have or don't have, puts you in a negative vibration and attracts to you more things to complain about. Whatever you focus on and give your energy and attention to, will grow and increase in your life. Being grateful in advance before you see any manifestation of your desire is an expression of faith.

Appreciation means to increase in value. Whenever we appreciate the people and the possessions in our lives they tend to go up in value in our estimation, when we fail to appreciate them they tend to go down in value. Donald Trump who made his billions mainly in real estate said, "If you appreciate your property, your property will appreciate for you." I found it interesting when I discovered that the Trump family were all brought up in New York and attended the Church where Norman Vincent Peale was the minister. Peale is best known for his international bestselling book of over 15 million copies, "The Power of Positive Thinking." The young Donald Trump obviously didn't grow up with any hang ups over whether it was biblical or not to be rich, now that is the power of positive influence.

Even if we didn't have the benefit of having such good mentors and teachers to influence our thinking when we were growing up, we can be grateful that today more than ever there is an abundance of material available for us to feed our minds with positive beliefs, and it's not too late to turn things around and create the life of our dreams. In fact the moment we begin to be grateful, our energy shifts into a positive vibration, and when you start giving out positive vibes through your thoughts, your words and your feelings, all the good that belongs to you will begin to move in your direction, and as your gratitude goes out from you consistently, good things will come back to you consistently. This doesn't happen by chance, it happens according to law, **the law of attraction**.

> "When you feel grateful, you become great, and attract
> great things."
> —Plato—

The Power of Clarity

Confusion leads to frustration, clarity leads to fulfilment. When you get clear about what you *really* want in life, you have a blueprint from which you can begin to produce the manifestation. Every house that is built began in the mind's eye. No one starts to build without first having a blueprint to work from. Earl Nightingale used to say, "If you can tell me what you want, I can show you how to get it." One reason why many people don't have what they want in life is simply because they don't really know with clarity what it is that they want to have. Like someone getting into a taxi and giving different directions to the driver at the turn of every corner, they end up going around in circles for a while and then find themselves right back where they started. When our conscious mind sends conflicting instructions to our subconscious mind, there is no definite destination or goal for it to begin to move you towards. But whenever you get clear and definite about *what* you want, and *why* you want it, the *how* to get it will begin to reveal itself.

> "Write the vision. And make it plain on tablets. That he may run who reads it."
> —The Prophet Habakkuk—

Make the vision clear. Send a clear message to your subconscious mind of what you want and it will begin to move you towards its fulfilment. Send mixed messages and you'll get a mixture of results. Most people focus *more* on what they don't want, than they focus on what they do want. Their conversation is more about things that they don't want and then they wonder why it keeps on showing up time and time again in their lives.

Clarity is attractive on so many levels. Women are attracted to men who seem to know where they are going. Men are attracted to women who are doing more than just waiting around for a rich prince charming to show up to rescue them. In fact the whole world seems to make room for the one who knows where they are going, and who has a passion and a purpose for getting there.

DISCOVERY ALWAYS PRECEDES RECOVERY

"You are today the same you'll be five years from now except for two things:

The people you meet and the books you read.

The people you meet can't always be with you, but what you read in books can remain with you for a lifetime.

How often we hear of individuals who began a new era in their lives from the reading of a single book."

—Russell Conwell—

For the price of a book and the time it takes to read it, you can obtain the knowledge that someone else spent *years* of their life learning. **The wisdom of the ages** is stored in books, and it can be found by anyone who is willing to pay the price and make the effort to discover it. It *does* cost you something to get knowledge, it costs you time and money, but a *lack* of knowledge can cost you much more in the long run. Ignorance can turn out to be very expensive. Anyone who has something that you don't have usually *knows* something that you don't know. Benjamin Franklin said, "If you think education is expensive, try ignorance."

"Rich people constantly learn and grow, poor people think they already know."

—T. Harv Eker—

The top people in every field are constantly learning and improving their game, they have a commitment to continual personal growth and development. One of the main factors in learning is having a teachable spirit. It's a common thing for successful people to admire and respect other successful people, this is the attitude that causes them to absorb their wisdom and then produce the same kind of results in their own lives.

"Wisdom is the principle thing; therefore get wisdom.
And in all your getting, get understanding."
—King Solomon—

This book contains many years of searching and studying the universal laws and principles that govern life and happiness. Much of it has been received through association with wise and successful individuals who have lived throughout the ages. As you read and study the wisdom within it, may you make some great discoveries that bring about great recoveries in every area of your life.

SUMMARY

Human beings, by changing the inner attitudes of their minds, can change the outer aspects of their lives.

Your outer world is a reflection of your inner world.

Your mind is the control centre of your life.

Everything that is coming into your life, you are attracting into your life.

Whatever is *impressed* on the subconscious mind will be *expressed* in your life experience.

Gratitude will draw more things into your life to be grateful for.

Mindsets are transferable, even from one generation to another, whether it is a positive mindset or a negative mindset.

The moment we begin to move in the direction of becoming our potential we start to feel better about ourselves.

Whenever you get clear and definite about *what* you want, and *why* you want it, the *how* to get it will begin to reveal itself.

Great discoveries bring about great recoveries.

CHAPTER 2

THE SEVEN DIMENSIONS
OF A HEALTHY LIFE

First of all, let me congratulate you for having the courage to pick up and read this book. Every book that you have on your book shelf says something about your passion. Whether the books you have are read or unread also reveals something about your priorities in life. If you don't *have* a book shelf or if it is full of entertainment dvd's, magazines or just *stuff* in general, this also tells us something about you. To purchase a book with the subject of money in the title, takes courage. This is firstly because you are admitting to yourself that you *want* to improve your financial situation. And secondly you'll find that an even greater courage is required because of the reaction that you may receive from some other people, when they see the title of the book in your possession. It has been said that, "Money, is one of the most highly charged words in any language that uses the stuff." When the subject of money comes up, you will get a variety of reactions, and some of them will be very emotional. I think that people are far more interested in this *money* stuff than many are prepared to admit that they are.

Since there is an intended emphasis on **finding financial freedom** throughout this book, it is my desire in this chapter to make it clear that money is not the *only* blessing you will ever need in this life. Financial health is indeed only *one* of the dimensions of having a truly wealthy life. Each dimension of our health overlaps and is interconnected with all the others. We know that good physical health cannot be purchased with money. However there is still a connection between our financial health and our physical health. Generally speaking wherever there is poverty there is usually also poor living conditions which can contribute to ill health and ultimately having a shorter life span. Being in good mental health can also influence your physical health for the better. And it's just as true that constant worries and anxieties or even just simply having a mindset that expects to lose health in later years, will influence your body in that direction.

A HEALTHY LIFE BALANCE

We are holistic in nature and every part of us should be valued and nourished if we desire to have an abundant life in every way. Balance is the key that we are looking for and a healthy life balance will bring us true fulfilment in every area. To focus only on one or two areas to the degree that we are neglecting the others will have its consequences. Some are very "spiritual," but they are struggling financially to make it through to the end of every month. Other people have more than enough money to live in luxury for the rest of their lives, but they are broke spiritually and have no inner peace of mind. I believe we do not have to lose one in order to have the other, we can choose to have both. We can have both money and meaning in our lives. We can have both peace and prosperity.

ARE YOU WILLING TO PAY THE PRICE?

John C Maxwell in his book, "Put Your Dream to the Test," gives ten questions that we should ask about our dreams. One of those questions is, "The cost question." Am I willing to pay the price for my dream? Certainly there is a price for everything and sometimes the price is simply too high that we should *not* be prepared to pay it. If it is going to cost me my health or my marriage in order to have it, then not only do I refuse to pay that price, but there is something seriously wrong about this situation.

We shouldn't have to kill ourselves in order to get ahead financially. Neither is it necessary that we lose our peace or give up our clear conscience by doing anything that wrongs another person in order to win financially in the game of life. These are a couple of reasons why we have certain negative sayings about money. Like, "Well, money is not the most important thing in life. Or money can't buy you happiness. You have to work hard to get money. Money doesn't grow on trees, or money is the root of all evil."

When we have a dream, there will always be a price to pay in order to achieve it. If we think that we will have to work all the hours under the sun, or rob a bank or get involved in any other kind of illegal activity that could risk a prison sentence if we are caught, then in this context I too would rather choose to hold onto my health, my peace and a good clear conscience, and make the most of the money that I can obtain honestly and in a humane manner. If my financial dream is going to end up costing me my physical health, my mental and emotional health, or perhaps even my spiritual health, then that is too high a price to have to pay for it. I guess I'll just have to find myself another dream.

But I am persuaded that our dreams can be achieved for a reasonable price. And that we can all pay that price and even enjoy the journey. If we repeatedly say and believe that it's so difficult to be successful, then our subconscious mind will receive that affirmation as a command and make sure that it *is* difficult for us. **Our belief will create the experience in our lives**. One of the most valuable lessons I learned from Catherine Ponders teaching is the suggestion that we begin or end our affirmations with the phrase: "In an easy and relaxed manner, in a healthy and positive way."

Affirmations have a way of getting down on the inside of us. Whatever we *repeatedly* hear or say over and over, we will eventually believe. This is how we have come to believe everything that we currently believe. These words are powerful when you say them to yourself over and over. Easy—relaxed—healthy—positive. When you begin to say a new affirmation, it can feel awkward within you. This is because your old programme is in conflict with it. The old ingrained belief is that it's going to be anything *but* easy. It's going to be extremely hard. You definitely won't be relaxed, you'll be stressed out. And it's not going to be healthy, it's going to be a headache, you might even burn out and die with a heart attack. This internal dialogue is your sad, sorry, currently programmed belief talking. But if you will persist with the new affirmation, these powerful positive words will become your *new* programme, and you will begin to experience breakthrough into new territories. And you will be amazed that you really *can* enjoy *all* the great riches of life, in an easy and relaxed manner, and in a healthy and positive way.

After all, we do tend to function better when we are relaxed. Our talents flow easily when we are relaxed. If we are all tense or fearful our performance will be poor. In the work environment the old management style was to crack the whip and make threats of someone being fired in an attempt to get more productivity out of the workers. But now we've discovered that happy people will perform better and produce better quality work than those who are stressed out would ever be able to produce. You and I really do bring the best out of ourselves when we make up our mind that we will do the task ahead of us in and easy and relaxed manner, and in a healthy and positive way. Now let's look at the seven dimensions of a healthy life.

#1 PHYSICAL HEALTH.

High levels of health and energy are essential for enjoying life. If you were to visit your local hospital and find a billionaire lying there on a bed, dying with cancer, who offered to give you his entire net worth in exchange for your health, you would be extremely foolish to accept his offer. Good physical health is priceless. Your body is the physical house that you live in. And if it is so run down through neglect that its condition is beyond repair, you will simply have to move out. You need your body to carry you throughout your lifetime, so take good care of it, because it is the only one you've got.

There are two kinds of pain in life, the pain of self discipline and the pain of regret. Taking care of your body by giving it the appropriate amount of exercise and feeding it an appropriate diet of healthy food takes discipline. It can be painful at times choosing to visit the gym rather than choosing not to, but the rewards of exercise definitely outweigh the regrets that a lack of exercise can bring. While physical exercise and a healthy diet won't guarantee that you'll never be attacked by an illness, it does help to build your immune system which makes your resistance to it stronger. Choosing the pain of self discipline in the present is the less painful option, when compared to perhaps suffering the pain of regret later on.

While these steps toward physical health are mainly practical, there are also mental, emotional and spiritual influences on whether or not we are able to enjoy vibrant physical health.

#2 MENTAL HEALTH.

Many books have been written on each dimension of health alone. This is but a short discussion on each area for the purpose of establishing that our health is multi dimensional. Napoleon Hill wrote that, "A positive mental attitude is one of the great riches of life." **Every improvement in our lives begins with an improvement in our thinking.** Our state of mind will affect our physical health, our social health and definitely our financial health. Having a sound mind is priceless. Having peace of mind cannot be purchased with money, however having money does tend to contribute towards us having peace of mind.

> "Happier thoughts lead to essentially a happier biochemistry, a happier, healthier body. negative thoughts and stress have been shown to seriously degrade the body and the functioning of the brain, because it's our thoughts and emotions that are continuously reassembling, reorganising and re-creating our body."
>
> —Dr John Hagelin—

Our thoughts have a tremendous creative energy within them. When our thoughts are despondent in nature, we will create feelings of despondency within us, which then will radiate out from us and will produce results according to their kind. When we deliberately choose to focus the great energy of our thinking toward ideas of plenty, plenty of health, plenty of life, plenty of happiness and even plenty of money, we will lift our feelings accordingly.

> "Turn the great energy of your thinking toward ideas of plenty."
>
> —Catherine Ponder—

Don't let your mind become the devil's playground. It's *your* mind, and you are in charge of it. Your mind is like a garden, and you are the gardener. You have to pull the weeds, and you have to plant the flowers. Whatever you allow to take root in your mind, will begin to grow in your life. There are certain things that no one else can do for you. If you don't do it, it won't get done. No one else can think your thoughts for you. No one else can guard your mind for you. You have the God given right to a free will. Other people can encourage you, they can motivate you and inspire you, but ultimately the choice is yours.

The mind is like a muscle, it will develop when you feed and exercise it. Benjamin Franklin once said, "Empty the coins of your purse into your mind and your mind will fill your purse with coins." Whenever you invest in your financial intelligence it won't be long before you have recouped your investment and a whole lot more besides.

#3 SOCIAL HEALTH.

Human beings are social beings. Relationships can be both the most rewarding and the most challenging aspects of our lives.

Back in 1953 Dale Carnegie first published his book, "How to Win Friends and Influence People." And in 2008 there was a British comedy film produced starring Simon Pegg called, "How to Lose Friends and Alienate People." Despite the fact that Dale Carnegie's book has sold over sixteen million copies, many of us today are still far better at losing friends and alienating people than we are at winning friends and influencing them. One reason for this is that the relationship that you have with yourself is without a doubt the most important relationship in your life. You are the one person that you can't ever get away from. Everywhere you go, there you are.

When you have a healthy self love and acceptance in spite of all your imperfections, you are in a good position to be able to love and accept other people as well, in spite of all *their* imperfections. If you can enjoy your own company, there is a good chance that other people will be able to enjoy your company also. If you don't really like yourself, you probably won't like anyone else either. Life can be much more enjoyable when you like people. And one of the side effects of genuinely liking people is that they will be more inclined to like you too.

> "The entire law is summed up in a single command,
> Love your neighbour as yourself."
> —Saint Paul (Galatians 5:14)—

Contrary to popular opinion, the first person you really need to take good care of is you. If you haven't taken good care of yourself, you are not likely to be in any condition to be able to take care of anyone else either. Love your neighbour *as* yourself. You can't give out to others what you yourself don't have. Your own happiness is vital, if you are ever going to be able to make anyone else happy. How can anyone who is miserable themselves, bring any happiness into the life of someone else. If you are always trying to make other people happy at the expense of your own happiness, the end result will be unhappiness for everyone.

> "Looking out for number one, as directed by the Infinite,
> is really looking out for number two and is indeed the only
> way to permanently benefit number two."
> —Prentice Mulford—

It is liberating to realise that not everyone is going to like you or agree with you. Out of the seven billion people who are alive on planet earth today, not everyone is going to like you. The good news is that you don't *need* everyone liking you in order to be a success in life, just a few million would probably be sufficient. So find your *own* passion and do what *you* love and those who are like minded will love you, and the others can go and find someone else that they *do* like and are in agreement with. Trying to please everyone is a very frustrating task. If you are a singer or song writer, not everyone is going to like your style. Don't get upset about it, as long as *somebody* likes you, you can make it.

Can you believe it? Not everyone is going to like *my* style, or agree with what I have to say. But if I'm going to let that put me off, then I'd be as well giving up before I start. I have heard it said, "If you don't want to be criticised, just say nothing, do nothing and be nothing." But even then someone will probably criticise you for saying nothing, doing nothing and being nothing.

"Criticism is the contribution of the mediocre to the successful."

Don't waste your time and energy trying to defend yourself against your critics. Use all your energy and your time pursuing your passion and investing in the lives of those you love and who love you. Prioritise in your relationships. Invest your best energy in those who are most important to you. A wonderful lesson I learned a few years ago was, **learning to say no, without feeling guilty**. Sometimes it is extremely difficult to say no to people. Particularly if we have a deep seated addiction to having everyone's approval, or if the person we are saying no to is one of those people who don't like to hear the word no. They demand an *explanation* of *why* you are not able to do what *they* think you should do. I'm sure you've met the type.

You may be thinking, well if you knew what *my* boss was like you wouldn't say no, or if you knew what *my* sister was like you wouldn't be able to say no either. In order to try and keep the peace, I just do whatever I'm told. You know what's coming next if you hesitate to obey, it's the guilt trip. "After *all* that we've done for you, can't you just do this *one* small thing?" Yeah right, until the next small thing again tomorrow. Be aware of the tools of emotional manipulation. Recognise when someone is attempting to send you on a guilt trip simply in order to get you to do what *they* want. Manipulation through guilt is not an act of love it's an act of selfishness. Of course they will accuse *you* of being the one who's selfish, that's a sure way of making you feel guilty. Remember, whenever you say yes to anything, you are also saying no to something. You could be saying yes to something that is of lesser importance to you, and end up having to say no to something that is of *greater* importance to you. You have to be strong and courageous to say no, and to do so without feeling guilty.

It's a wonderful thing to be able to be assertive without being aggressive. Do not allow other people to run your life for you. Decide what you want and choose what you want, not what someone else wants you to have. If there is a no in your heart, don't say yes with your mouth just to try and keep someone else happy. If there is a yes in your heart, then you can go ahead and say yes with your mouth. Let your yes be yes, and your no, be no. Be self controlled, don't allow your life be controlled by other people.

There is obviously a healthy control as well as an unhealthy control. Take a parents relationship with their children for example. There *is* a time for parents to make decisions on their children's behalf, but when the children become adults, it is not so appropriate for parents to *still* be making decisions for them.

To have good social health, be free to be yourself and allow others the freedom to be who they are, then they will *want* to have your company, and they will *enjoy* having you around. Allow others to have their own opinions, and expect them to allow you to have your own opinions as well.

"If I'm going to be free, I've got to be me. Not the me that someone else thinks I should be, but the me that I was created to be."

—Unknown—

#4 VOCATIONAL HEALTH.

"Think of work as vocation. It comes from the latin word for calling, which comes from the word for voice. In those meanings it touches on what work really should be. It should be something that calls to you as something you want to do, and it should be something that gives voice to who you are and what you want to say to the world. It is something that you choose because of what it allows you to say with your life."

—Kent Nerburn—

In interviews with outstanding successful men and women throughout history, they all seem to have this thing in common, they all knew exactly what they wanted to achieve and they had a burning desire to achieve it. Each of us has the potential within us to achieve great things with our own unique gifts and talents, to contribute something of value to the world and be rewarded in return for it. Human beings are most fulfilled and happy when they are using their gifts, abilities and talents doing what they love and enjoy.

This is one reason why many people are so looking forward to retirement, because they have been stuck in jobs that they don't enjoy for years. People who are doing what they are passionate about don't seem to *want* to retire. I believe it was Henry ford who said, "I've never worked a day in my life, it was all just my hobby." He arrived at work before anyone else and was the last to leave at the end of the day. Work to some people is a curse and devilish, to others it is a blessing and divine. Doing what you love and being paid well for doing it, is one of the great riches of life.

"Don't ask what the world needs. Ask what makes you come alive, and go do it. Because what the world needs is people who have come alive."

—Howard Thurman—

What would you like to be doing? What kind of work could really turn on the enthusiasm inside you? **What makes *you* come alive?** You will never be as good at anything as you will be when you are doing something that stirs your passion. You will learn much easier when you are genuinely interested in the subject. We spend so many hours of our day at the workplace, so many days of our week, so many weeks in the year and so many years of our life. What a blessing it is to enjoy your work, and to enjoy the people you are working with. Life is too short to spend it in dissatisfying labour.

It's not always about which job pays the highest salary either. As much as I appreciate financial freedom and in the following chapters do emphasise the value of it, I personally wouldn't always choose the highest paying position if I was going to be miserable all day long in it. That said, working with our gifts and talents is also the primary means by which we are rewarded financially, so it is in our own interests that we discover our best fitted type of vocation and develop our potential for service there. We are paid according to the amount of value that we bring to the marketplace. To increase our pay, we simply have to increase the value that we are contributing.

Perhaps your current line of work is not exactly your dream job. Realise that this too shall pass, and that this is only a season which can last as long or as short as you decide. Everything in your life will change for the better, if you do. This is the aim of the contents of this book. To stir up the gifts within you, and to make you aware that you are already far more capable than perhaps you realise, and that **you have within you everything you need for achieving the life of your dreams**. By the time you are finished reading this book, I am certain that you won't be in the same state of mind that you were when you first began.

It is my aim to talk to the winner in you. Dr Mike Murdock says that, "Every man has a king and a fool in him and the one that you talk to is the one that will talk back." I aim to talk to the king in you. I'm talking about your higher self. That's what self help and personal development is all about. Growing into your potential and becoming the most magnificent version of yourself. One year from now, you could be in an entirely different set up from where you are today. In a completely different line of work, with new and enjoyable relationships, higher levels of health and energy and a whole new outlook on life, and it will all be because you changed your thinking concerning what was possible for you.

Everyday can be a great day. You can wake up in the morning excited about the day ahead. That's the way life is meant to be. And that's the way your life is going to be, when you learn and live the success principles revealed in the pages ahead. The best days of your life are not behind you, they are ahead of you. Enjoy the journey.

#5 SPIRITUAL HEALTH.

It has been said that man is not a physical being having a spiritual experience he is a spiritual being having a physical experience. Being spiritual does not equal being religious. Some people are spiritual but not very religious, others are religious but not very spiritual, and there are those who are both religious and spiritual. Generally speaking, when we think of spiritual matters, we immediately think of our beliefs concerning God. Allow me to shoot straight with you right from the very beginning. It *is* absolutely my intention to convert you while you are reading this book. To convert means to *change* and I think all of us could benefit from some positive changes in our lives. If your concept of God and religion is one that *prevents* you from enjoying the abundant life in every area including your financial life, then I am definitely going to try to convert you.

Converting the soul means renewing the mind. And a renewed mind will produce a renewed life. A prosperous soul is required for having a prosperous life. Converting the soul is a process, it doesn't happen overnight. After all, you didn't get to where you are now overnight. It has taken many years for some of us to get as messed up in our thinking as we are right now. Dr Mike Murdock told of how a religious woman approached him and said indignantly, "God made me the way I am." He replied, "No way, He made you the way you *were*, and you have *become* the way you are." It is true that God loves us and accepts us the way we are, but He loves us *too* much to leave us the way we are. However He is a gentleman, and will only help us with His wisdom and instruction, if we *want* to be helped. There is a Chinese proverb that says, "When the student is ready, the teacher will appear."

It is a wonderful liberation when we realise that **God is not against our success and prosperity in life.** The scriptures reveal that He will even *assist* us in achieving it, if we will allow Him to do so.

> "Remember the Lord your God for it is He who gives you power to get wealth."
> —Deuteronomy 8:18—

A healthy spiritual life will increase and sharpen your discernment. And as you pay more attention to your inner intuition, you will make more wise choices which will ultimately bring better results. As they say, "An ounce of intuition is better than a pound of tuition." The early chapters in this book deal more with the psychological, mental, emotional and practical laws that govern life prosperity. The later chapters reveal the *advanced* laws, which are of a spiritual nature. Spiritual laws are higher laws, they have authority *over* natural laws, and when they are activated they can produce *supernatural* progress in our lives. God is the source of all life, health, wisdom and wealth. Therefore it would obviously benefit us to be connected to Him in relationship rather than to be disconnected from Him. Spiritual blessing is an *empowerment* from heaven, and when it gets on your life, whatever you put your hands to, shall prosper.

#6 RECREATIONAL HEALTH.

In all our pursuits in life, let us remember to enjoy the journey. It's not only about the destination, it's also about having a great trip on the way to reaching it. If you are one of those who feel guilty taking a day off, then you need an increase of recreational health. Even the word recreation when broken down means re-creation. When you give yourself a break and rest a while, your energy is replenished, your body is revived and your vision can be re-created with fresh insight.

Even God took a day off and rested. I don't think it was because He was tired, but rather that He sat back and appreciated what His labour had produced. It's strange how some people can't seem to get *started* working, and others just can't seem to stop. Just as we don't live to eat, but rather we eat to live, neither should we live to work, but rather we work to live. Perhaps it's time to take a vacation. Take time to appreciate what your labour has produced and enjoy the fruit of the work of your hands.

Life is meant to be fun. We see it that way when we are children. But when we become adults, it's easy to get caught up in the seriousness of life, with all our responsibilities and somehow the fun side can be diminished. In order to have a healthy life balance, we can pursue finances and fulfilment, without giving up on having fun.

I read recently about the difference between balance and harmony. In an orchestra for example, all the instruments are not constantly playing at the same level. They are all *involved* but certain instruments will come out to the forefront for a period. The brass section will be given the centre stage and then they will pull back for the stringed instruments to take over. Then they will quieten down to allow perhaps the flute to come to the centre of attention for a while. All the instruments are in harmony together but not all constantly playing at the same volume.

In our lives we can have certain aspects that have to take the centre stage for a period. Studying for an exam can be the central focus for a while even to the apparent neglect of other things. But when the exam is over we can get back to paying attention to the things we neglected for a while. We don't need to feel guilty about giving something more attention than usual for a season if that's what's needed at the time. Ultimately we are aiming for harmony and things will balance out eventually. We have to focus on our work lives at certain seasons, but there is also a season for relaxing, resting and recreation.

#7 FINANCIAL HEALTH.

"Money, it turned out, was exactly like sex. You thought
of nothing else if you didn't have it, and thought of other
things if you did"
—James Baldwin—

We all have certain beliefs, attitudes and behaviours towards money which can be the very reasons why we are struggling financially. A doctor in America said that he would have few patients if it were not for financial problems which cause us anxiety, worry and stress, all of which can lead to ill health. **Freedom from money worries has more rewards than just the material things you are in a position to be able to afford.** Money is used as a means of exchange. Not only can it be exchanged for material *things*, but pleasant *experiences* in life can be yours if you have sufficient money to pay the price for them. It is to our advantage to have a friendly, positive attitude towards money. If we respect and appreciate it, money will be friendly towards us.

"When your thinking becomes friendly towards prosperity, Prosperity will become friendly towards you."
—Catherine Ponder—

PRACTICAL PRINCIPLES FOR MONEY MANAGEMENT

Life success is achieved by having the proper life balance. We are spiritual, intellectual and emotional in our inner being, and it is true that our inner world creates our outer world. However, there are practical steps to take as well in order to reach our goals in life.

THE SOLUTION TO YOUR MONEY PROBLEMS

Lots of financial advice we hear is about helping us to save money and this is good, we would all be much better off if we used more wisdom in managing what we already have. One personal development trainer opens his success seminars by saying, "How many of you would like to double your income?" Hands go up all over the room. Some people even cheer and shout with enthusiasm. Then he asks, "How many *think* that doubling their income would solve all their financial problems?" Again the audience responds positively. Next question, "How many from the time you began working have *already* doubled your income?" Again almost all the hands in the room go up. Then the trainer makes his point. If doubling your income would solve all your financial problems, then your problems would already be solved as most of you have already doubled or even trebled your income since the time you began working.

More money coming in doesn't always solve our money problems. If we mismanage what we currently have, it is very likely that if we had twice as much coming in we would mismanage that also. Some people are earning two or three times as much as you are on a monthly basis, but they are as broke as the ten commandments. If we are faithful with little, we will also be faithful with much, and if we are foolish with little, we will also be foolish with much.

My Financial Freedom Story

> "Train up a child in the way he should go, and when he
> is old he will not depart from it. The rich rule over the poor
> and the borrower is servant to the lender."
> —King Solomon—

I consider myself fortunate to have had a Dad who taught me at an early age the principles of money management. I remember when I was about 14 years old and a couple of hairs began to appear on my chin, at which point I thought I would need to begin shaving soon on a regular basis. My Dad had two electric shavers, and at that time I received a couple of pounds pocket money each week. I thought it would be a good idea to buy my Dad's old electric shaver from him. He explained that the shaver brand new would cost about £6, but since it was 2nd hand, he would sell it to me for just £3, to which I agreed. I used the shaver once and then realised after two weeks went by and no further hairs had yet appeared on my chin, that I didn't really *need* the shaver after all, and I could think of several other alternatives to spend the money on. So I suggested selling the shaver back to dad.

He explained that it was now 3rd hand and was only worth £2.50. My Mother overheard and sympathetically said, "Awe, that's a shame give him the £3 back." To which my Dad replied, "I'm training the boy." Well, £2.50 was all I got for it and I didn't at the time see it as training, but more that my Dad was tight and was out to make a 50 pence profit from his 14 year old son.

On another occasion when my birthday was approaching I expressed an interest in a stereo record player. (I'm giving my age away here.) Dad advised that this would cost more than they had planned to spend on me for my birthday, but if I saved my pocket money from now until my birthday arrived, I would have saved enough to pay the difference in price. This happened on several occasions including my request for a bike at Christmas time. I used to say that my Dad got me half a bike for Christmas, as I paid for the other half myself. Some would laugh and accuse Dad of being miserable, but as I grew older I began to practice the principle of saving for something I desired in the future.

After passing my driving test in my early 20's, I borrowed money from Dad to purchase my first two cars. After almost paying back the loan on the second car, I was intending to repeat the same process for the next one, but Dad had a different idea. He said, "There's nothing wrong with the car that you have now, it's a good car and still has plenty of miles left in it. Why don't you hold onto it, and the money you would normally be paying back on a loan, put that into an account every month, and after two years or so, you'll be able to buy your next car without having to borrow from anyone?" This initially was *not* what I wanted to hear, however, I took his advice and from that time on, I have been paying cash for my cars. While many colleagues were taking out bank loans or finance agreements to buy their cars and paying back the loan with interest for somewhere between two and five years, mine was paid for with cash in full on the first day. (Thank you, Dad.)

Don't misunderstand me, Dad didn't pay for it, I paid for it, Dad just showed me how to do it. A good Dad will buy it for you. A *great* Dad will teach you how to buy it yourself.

Over the years I have saved a fortune in interest. Having left school at age 16 and started working in a butcher shop. A friend of mine about the same age was considering moving out from his parent's house and buying his own flat, this was when I first got some information about mortgages. When I saw how much interest the bank was charging on their loan, I had this thought, "Wouldn't it be *great* to be able to buy a house without a mortgage?" I was getting myself ready to graduate and move up the ladder from record players and bikes and cars, now I'm thinking about going for the big one, a house. And to cut a long story short, before I reached my 30th birthday, I had bought my first house and paid cash for it. From then until now I have purchased four properties and paid cash for them on each occasion.

Now, whoever it was who said that money doesn't make you happy, lied. Believe me, it feels real good to visit a brand new housing estate, view the show house and be able to say, "I'll take this one", knowing that you don't have to borrow a penny from anyone.

So what credentials do I have to be giving any advice on money management? These are my credentials. Some financial advisers are in more debt themselves than the people who are paying them for advice are. It's always wise to check out the *results* in the personal lives of those who are offering you advice. I assure you, it feels *real* good to put your head on the pillow at night and know that your house is paid for. Being debt free is a wonderful place to be. Not only has my Dad's advice saved me a lot on interest payments, but it has saved me a lot of stress as well.

Most people spend everything they earn and a little bit more on credit cards. Statistics tell us that most families are only two pay checks away from potential homelessness. The buy now and pay later mentality has got us trapped in indebtedness, and as Solomon said, "The borrower is servant to the lender." Being unable to delay immediate gratification keeps the debt cycle going. For me personally, my pursuit of financial independence is not so much about the money, it's about the freedom. I do not share my experience to brag, but to show that even without a great formal education, and without a highly paid career, anyone of average intelligence even earning an average income can become financially free, if only they will learn how to manage wisely what they have. It's not really about how much you make, but rather about how much you keep and invest that determines your financial future.

The English writer C. Northcote Parkinson many years ago introduced us to what is now called Parkinson's law. Which is that, expenses always rise to meet income. Whenever people get an increase in income, they usually increase their spending as well, taking on more financial commitments. This way no matter how much they make, there never seems to be enough left over at the end of the month. The only way to ever become financially free is to drive a wedge between your income and your expenditure and then save and invest the difference.

> "The main reason people struggle financially is because
> they have spent years in school but learned nothing about
> money. The result is that people learn to work for money . . .
> but never learn to have money work for them."
> —Robert Kiyosaki—

THE RICHEST MAN IN BABYLON

One of the all time greatest books on money management is, "The Richest Man in Babylon" which was written in 1926 by George S.

Clason. One golden nugget of advice is this. "For every ten coins thou placest within thy purse, take out for use but nine. Thy purse will start to fatten at once and its increasing weight will feel good in thy hand and bring satisfaction to thy soul."

It's easy to get yourself into debt if you only feel happy when you are spending money. If you are feeling a bit down, go out and buy yourself something nice and that will make you feel better. It's even got a name for it, "Retail therapy." The main problem is that if you are spending money on credit, a few weeks later when the bill comes in, you can end up feeling bad again, and so you have to go out and buy something else just to cheer yourself up. This of course isn't going to help you reach your goal of debt freedom. Here is the solution. You have to disconnect your happiness wire from your spending wire, and reconnect it to your saving wire. Previously you would only be happy when you are spending, but now you only get happy when you are saving money. As the writer mentioned above says, "Thy purse will start to fatten at once and its increasing weight will feel good in thy hand." When your happiness wire is connected to your saving wire, you *don't* feel good when you are spending money, but you feel *great* every time your savings and investments are increasing.

This is good for a while to break the over spending pattern, but we have to watch that we don't let our happiness wire get so stuck on saving, that it stays there permanently and when we have reached the stage of being able to treat ourselves and others, we are unable to do so. Some people end up miserable anytime they have to spend money. We are holistic in nature. Our responsible self is fulfilled when we are saving and investing for our future, but the fun-seeking part of us isn't. There has to be a proper balance, or our pleasure seeking side could end up rebelling and sabotaging our efforts by blowing everything we have put aside. However if we deny our responsible self expression, not only will we never be financially free but even all the things we buy will no longer make us feel happy or fulfilled deep down on the inside. There is an appropriate time to save, and there is an appropriate time to spend, and it takes wisdom to know which is which.

PERSISTENCE IS THE KEY TO THE BREAKTHROUGH

Perhaps you have heard or read previously about financial prosperity principles and the law of attraction and have not yet seen much change in your outward conditions, don't give up. Everyone who persists has their breakthrough moment. To experience a dramatic change financially, there has to be a dramatic change in our beliefs and in our thinking about finances, and this takes time. Persistence is the key to the breakthrough, just keep with the programme and the tide will begin to turn in your favour. For some people, all that is required is a few minor adjustments and suddenly things will begin to change for the better. The majority of those who achieve financial freedom didn't do so overnight, It's the minority who get rich quick, and usually they get broke again just as quick.

HOW TO DEVELOP A PROSPERITY CONSCIOUSNESS

There are more barriers internally than there are externally. Just about every financial trainer or coach will say that wealth is first of all a mindset. Just as a thermostat which is set at a certain temperature will keep the room from going over or under that setting, so will our own internal mindset keep our achievements from rising higher or falling lower than we have decided we are capable of. **Prosperous thinking will begin to open up the way for prosperous results**.

"What you radiate outward in your thoughts, feelings,
mental pictures and words you attract into your life."
—Catherine Ponder—

How do you feel about someone else's success? Your reaction is very important. If upon seeing or hearing of someone else's promotion or when a friend has an opportunity to increase financially, you become envious and jealous of them, you are sending out a negative vibe regarding financial increase and will attract back events and situations that are in harmony with your vibration of lack. But if you can get happy for them and celebrate as though it were happening for you, you are identifying with their success and sending out the signal that you are on the same frequency as they are, so a similar opportunity, and maybe something even better will come looking for you also. These universal principles will help you to attract more money into your life, recession or no recession.

When you **download a new financial freedom programme into your subconscious mind**, this will become your new *mindset* and your life will begin to move into alignment with it. The more you feed your mind with principles and pictures of abundance, the more your prosperity consciousness will grow. The more you do practically by saving and wisely investing your money, and the more you begin to emotionally feel positive about money, the more you will begin to attract money making ideas and opportunities. In relation to money we could say that spending means subtraction, saving means addition, and investing means multiplication. This section covers mainly the saving aspect which allows you to operate in addition. The chapters ahead will lift us into another dimension of money multiplication.

SUMMARY

There are two kinds of pain in life, the pain of self discipline and the pain of regret.

Money is not the *only* blessing you will ever need in this life. Financial health is indeed only *one* of the dimensions of having a truly wealthy life.

We all have certain beliefs, attitudes and behaviours towards money which can be the very reasons why we are struggling financially.

More money coming in doesn't always solve our money problems. If we mismanage what we currently have, it's very likely that if we had twice as much coming in we would mismanage that also.

To experience a dramatic change financially, there has to be a dramatic change in our beliefs and in our thinking about finances.

The only way to become financially free is to drive a wedge between your income and your expenditure and then save and invest the difference.

The majority of those who achieve financial freedom didn't do so overnight, It's the minority who get rich quick, and usually they get broke again just as quick.

Prosperous thinking will begin to open up the way for prosperous results.

The more you feed your mind with principles and pictures of abundance, the more your prosperity consciousness will grow.

CHAPTER 3

THE FIVE STEPS OF THE CREATION PROCESS

This is a wonderful time to be alive. There has never been a time in history where there has been so much information available and so easily accessible than there is today. The principles contained within the pages ahead have produced success in many different fields of ambition throughout history. Success is predictable and so is failure. **A successful life doesn't happen by chance, it happens by choice.** Knowledge is available for all, and those who consider it valuable will pursue it. Fortunately for us we do not have to reinvent the wheel, it has already been invented. And the knowledge of how to win in life has already been discovered and captured. We do not have to start our search from scratch for **we have been left an inheritance** from those who have gone before us. Whether we realise it or not we *are* creating our own future, both collectively and individually. We have been given the tools and the authority to build, so let's make it a masterpiece.

"What lies behind us and what lies before us are tiny matters compared to what lies within us."
—Ralph Waldo Emerson—

THE FIRST STEP IN THE CREATION PROCESS IS TO IDEALISE.

As Stephen Covey puts it, "Begin with the end in mind." Everything begins with an idea. Every creation and invention that we have and use today began with an *idea* in someone's mind. The light bulb, the telephone, the car and the airplane, the internet, the laptop and even the chair you are sitting on all began with an idea in the mind. Can you imagine that five years from now you are living your ideal life? You are the kind of person that you want to be, you are doing the kind of things that you want to do, and you have the kind of things that you want to have. What does your ideal life look like?

"If you can dream it, you can do it"
—Walt Disney—

WHAT DO YOU REALLY WANT?

If there were no limitations and you were allowed to dream, what would your ideal life be like? Often our past programming starts telling us to be "realistic" and before we know it we've given up on our dreams before we even begin. If we do manage to press through, it's usually someone else's opinion that influences us to give up too soon. Perhaps it is because others see in you a courage that they don't have in themselves, and won't feel as bad about not achieving *their* dreams if you don't achieve yours either. Although more often than not it is simply that they are well meaning and trying to protect you from possible disappointment, but going through life without even trying to win is the biggest disappointment of all.

Without trying to figure out *how* it's going to happen at this stage, begin to imagine your ideal life. Remember everything created began with an idea. You and I are in the creation process everyday of our lives. We are creative beings, created in the image and likeness of the creator Himself, we are His offspring. The creator God created man a creative being.

Everyone is creating something. Some are creating problems for themselves and others, while some are working on creating solutions for problems to help make people's lives better and richer. We are living in today the *results* of what we created yesterday, and we will experience tomorrow the results of what we are creating today. Our own self limiting beliefs are creating boundaries and barriers in our lives.

> "The boundaries of your life are not on the outside. The boundaries of your life are on the *inside* of you."
> —Dr Bill Winston—
> Author of: "Transform your thinking, Transform your life."

It is your inner world that is creating your outer world. Most people are living by default rather than by design. Very few people know exactly what they want in life, like Zig Ziglar says, "Most people are wandering generalities rather than meaningful specifics." Knowing what you want in life will greatly increase the possibility of your achieving it.

WHAT DOES SUCCESS MEAN TO YOU?

Decide and define what success means to you. Be honest with yourself, sometimes we kid ourselves on that we are not really interested in financial success, but then we are jealous, envious and critical of others who have the things that we tried to pretend to ourselves and others that we didn't want. Of course success is more than material and financial, but about 80 percent of the population are stressed out and preoccupied worrying about money matters. Money is not the root of all evil, but the lack of money is a root of all kinds of evil. Many health problems and relationship problems are all *caused* by money worries, so include financial freedom in the plan for your ideal life. Ideally we can have both good health and wealth, we can enjoy peace and prosperity.

The ideal life would surely include self expression through meaningful work, freedom from financial worries, high levels of health and energy and happy relationships with others. Allow yourself to dream. Give yourself permission to imagine the good life. This then becomes the blueprint from which you can begin to build. The first step in the creation process is to idealise.

THE SECOND STEP IS TO VISUALISE.

"Where there is no vision the people perish."
—King Solomon—

We all have a marvellous mind which can either be our greatest asset for success or our greatest hindrance and the main cause of our failures and frustrations in life. The choice is ours. **Your mind can be your best friend or your worst enemy**. We are responsible for what we permit to take root in the garden of our mind. You are the custodian of your thought life, and your life will always move in the direction of your most dominant thoughts.

THE POWER OF IMAGINATION

One of the faculties of the mind is the memory, another is the imagination. Your memory replays your past, your imagination pre-plays your future. Albert Einstein said, "Imagination is everything, it is the *preview* of life's coming attractions." The most powerful nation on earth today is the imagination.

> "Nothing they have imagined to do will be withheld
> from them."
> —Genesis 11:6—

To visualise is to bring an image before the mind's eye. Everyone visualizes. The mind thinks in pictures. If you just can't see yourself doing it, it's unlikely that you ever will. I heard a friend say, "I just can't see myself *ever* owning a car like that." Well there's not much chance that they will, because we have to be able to *see* it if we are ever going to *be* it.

Vision is powerful. When you habitually visualise it, you will materialise it, whatever *it* may be, good or bad. Napoleon Hill said, "Whatever the mind of man can conceive and believe it can achieve." Many people would agree about the dangers of negative thinking or mentally rehearsing acts of violence, and yet they often belittle the idea that positive thinking will bring positive results. These are simply two sides of the same coin, if it works negatively, it will also work positively. Thoughts become things.

"Logic will get you from A to B. Imagination will take you everywhere."

—Albert Einstein—

YOUR SELF IMAGE

You will never outperform the image you have of yourself. You always act in a manner consistent with the person you think you are. The way you see yourself determines your outward behaviour. When the children of Israel went to spy out the promised land, ten out of the twelve spies came back with this report.

"There we saw the giants, and we were like grasshoppers in our own sight, and so we were in their sight."

—Numbers 13:33—

The way you see yourself, determines how others see you. They saw themselves as small, weak and inferior. It's a strange thing that others tend to pick up from you the way you feel about yourself. If you don't like yourself, it's unlikely that anyone else will. A healthy self concept is the foundation of a healthy life. If you can enjoy your own company, other people will probably enjoy your company as well. Your higher self is the most magnificent version of you. Within all of us there is the best of us and the worst of us. We are all living on the scale somewhere in between the two extremes. Your higher self is amazing, and that's your real self. Maybe hurts and disappointments have caused you to respond negatively and you are currently living far from the most magnificent version of you. Fortunately **change is simply a matter of choice**. Get a vision of yourself at your best. The law of concentration says that whatever you *focus* on will increase and grow in your experience.

Set a new goal for yourself and visualise yourself with the desired end result. See yourself enjoying good health, wealth and happiness. **Programme your mind for success and you will begin to attract it.** Your subconscious mind works in ways beyond your understanding to bring about whatever you plant within it, so be good to yourself, and think magnificent thoughts.

"Visualise this thing that you want. See it, feel it, believe in it. Make your mental blueprint, and begin to build."
—Robert Collier—

THE THIRD STEP IN THE CREATION PROCESS IS TO EMOTIONALISE

"Whatsoever things you desire when you pray, believe that you have received them and you shall have them."
—Mark 11:24—

Believe that you *have* received them. This is present tense, not future tense. If we believe that we *will* receive sometime in the future, that tells our subconscious mind that we don't have it *now*. When you believe that you *have* received you get happy like it's already yours, you celebrate like it's already done. You start to **be thankful and grateful in advance of the manifestation**, this gets you in alignment for receiving. We have to get *emotionally* involved in our dream. How would you *feel* if you had today the answer to your prayers?

FAITH AND FEELINGS

It's often said that we live by our faith not by our feelings. However it's important to know that we have two sets of feelings, physical and spiritual. Our physical feelings come from our outward man, that is our body, and are based on what we see and feel in the physical and material world through our physical senses. Our spiritual feelings are from within us, in our inward man, and are based on what we believe in our hearts. That's why you can get excited in advance of seeing any outward change in your situation, because your inner being has conceived something and as far as your belief is concerned, you've already got it. So let your inner being express its emotions and get involved with your dream. **It's really the *feeling* that creates the power of attraction.** If your answer comes to you and you are feeling miserable and full of doubt and unbelief, it will think it's got the wrong address and move on to someone else. **You've got to be in harmony with it for it to come to you**. The *feeling* of success produces success and the *feeling* of failure just produces more failure. The feeling of wealth produces wealth, and the feeling of lack produces more lack.

> "There is a world within—a world of thought and feeling
> and power, of light and beauty, and although invisible, it's
> forces are mighty."
> —Charles Hannel—

Some people think, that's a lot of mumbo jumbo, all that matters is taking action. Well, taking action certainly is important, however if you do all the right things outwardly, but inwardly you are thinking how hard it is to get ahead and deep down you expect to fail, your inner belief and feeling will *override* your outward actions and produce difficulties and obstacles and eventually failure, then you'll say to yourself, I just knew this wouldn't work out.

The Science of Getting Rich

In 1910 Wallace Wattles wrote a book called, "The Science of Getting Rich," in which he said, "You don't get rich by doing certain things, you get rich by doing things in a certain way." That's one of the reasons why there are many highly paid people, in good careers who are up to their eyeballs in debt, and there are others in the very same job, working for the very same company who are debt free and always have a surplus.

It isn't the type of business you are in that guarantees your success, it is more about the spirit and mentality in which you *do* business that makes for success or failure. When you take the right action in the right frame of mind, you have the winning combination. Outward action, backed up with the inner conviction of success will produce successful results.

Your feelings will always follow your thoughts. It is impossible to be thinking negative thoughts and be feeling good at the same time, and equally impossible to be thinking positive thoughts and be feeling miserable at the same time. When you are feeling down, just pause and ask yourself, what have I been thinking about for the last while, and you'll discover that **your negative thoughts have been creating your negative feelings**. If you will take charge of your thinking and on purpose begin to think about things of good report, you will find that your feelings will begin to change for the better. It certainly is amazing how when you are feeling good and sending out those good feeling vibes, that the entire day can turn out to be a great one.

"Through your ability to think and feel, you have dominion over all creation."
—Neville Goddard—

It is equally true that when you are feeling miserable and negative, the day just seems to go from bad to worse. **You are not the victim, you are the creator**. A bad day didn't just come along looking especially for you. Your habitual thought patterns are *creating* your feelings, and your feelings are determining whether you are in a positive or a negative vibration. Nothing can come into your experience unless you are mentally in harmony with it. Your thoughts and your feelings are creating your day for you, and you can create a lousy day for yourself or you can create a wonderful day, and if you'll get into the habit of it, you'll create a wonderful life. The choice is yours. **Mastery over your emotions will bring great rewards into your experience**.

"Whatever things are true, whatever things are noble, whatever things are just, whatever things are pure, whatever things are lovely, whatever things are of good report, if there is any virtue and if there is anything praiseworthy, think on these things."
—Philippians 4:8—

THE 4TH STEP IS TO VERBALISE.

This is where the power of affirmations comes into play. When you and I want to create something in our world, our mouths will have to get involved.

"Death and life are in the power of the tongue."

—King Solomon—

Previously we saw that we are creative beings for we were created in the image and likeness of our creator Himself. In the Genesis account of creation we read that God said, "Let there be light, and there was light." The chapter goes on, and God said . . . and God said . . . and God said. Whenever God wanted to create something, He said something. "Let there be . . . . and it was so." At the end of the chapter in verse 31, God *saw* all that He had made, and it was very good. God saw everything that He had *said*.

THE POWER OF YOUR WORDS

Our words are like capsules containing creative ability when our words are filled with conviction and belief. If our words do not contain much passion and emotion, they are merely "empty words" void of any creative substance. The problem is that many of our negative words *are* filled with conviction, frustration and emotion and they are not creating for us the kind of results or experiences that we *want* to have. If we want to see change in our lives, we will have to retrain ourselves to stop speaking negative words over our lives and futures, and then to start deliberately speaking positive words instead. **Your words are creating *your* world.**

"You will also declare a thing, and it will be established for you."

—Job 22:28—

Have you ever deliberately paid attention to the words you speak or the words you hear others speaking? It's actually quite shocking to hear how *negative* our vocabulary is. These are some of the phrases you'll hear.

"My feet are killing me."

"My back is killing me."

"That was so funny, I was killing myself laughing."

"That old car will be the death of me yet."

"If anything bad is going to happen it always seems to happen to me."

"Well I guess that just runs in our family.

Speaking foolish words can run in a family also. Sayings and phrases can be passed on to the next generation. Illness and weakness can show up generation after generation not necessarily because it's in the genes, but sometimes it's simply because we speak it over ourselves. Why is there so much death in our vocabulary? No wonder so many people's lives are cut short. **The words that we speak can either be a blessing or a curse to us.** Some people like to play the role of the victim and blame anything and everything else for their troubles, but don't think for a moment that *they* could be responsible for what's showing up in *their* world. Could it be that much of the trouble and even the tragedy in our world, *we* have at least contributed to it by speaking it into being? I don't think it has really dawned on us just how much authority in the earth we have been given.

"You and I go through life with an awesome power-like fire or electricity or nuclear energy—right under our noses, one that can produce death or life, depending on how it is used."

—Joyce Meyer—

CONFESSION BRINGS POSSESSION

This law of creation is no respecter of persons. It is like the soil that will produce whatever kind of seed you plant in it. If you don't like the harvest you are reaping, all you have to do is change the kind of seed you are sowing. You can be the one who starts the turnaround in your family. Speak blessing over your life and your future. If you are consistently talking defeat, then defeat will be produced. When you speak words of doubt and fear, you send your voice into your own subconscious mind and plant seeds of doubt and fear. So begin to verbalise the good that you desire. Declare it, decree it, and make a demand on it and it will be established for you. There is power in your words. Confession brings possession.

> "Whosoever shall say unto this mountain, be thou removed and be cast into the sea, and shall not doubt in his heart but shall believe that those things which he saith shall come to pass, he shall have whatsoever he saith."
> —Mark 11:23—

THE 5TH STEP IN THE CREATION PROCESS IS TO MATERIALISE

The Law of Manifestation

When you *idealise* it and you *visualise* it. You *emotionalise* it and you *verbalise* it, you will *materialise* it. It's only a matter of time. It's **the law** of manifestation. Whatever you focus on will expand and grow in your experience. **Never underestimate the power within you**. Universal laws are always working and are as faithful and unchanging as the one who created them. Whenever anyone has a prolonged habitual and emotionalised pattern of thinking, something is going to manifest out of those thought patterns. When your mind is made up and set on the desired outcome, and your subconscious has received the instruction, from then on your course of action will be directed and controlled by the wonder working power within you. It simply just *has* to happen.

> Your decision will be right. There will only be right action because you are under a subjective compulsion to do the right thing. I use the word compulsion because the law of the subconscious is compulsion.
>
> —Dr Joseph Murphy—

The Law of Seedtime and Harvest

Just as surely as a pregnant woman will give birth when her time has come, you will give birth to whatever you have *conceived* on the inside of you. So get pregnant with a great vision for your life. Grow that baby on the inside of you, and don't let doubt or discouragement abort your dreams. The more you feed and nourish the dream within you, the bigger it will grow, until it no longer can remain in the unseen realm, it has outgrown that space and must enter into the next dimension.

> "The vision is for an appointed time, though it tarry, wait expectantly for it, it will surely come and not prove false."
>
> —The Prophet Habakkuk—

The Five Steps Of The Creation Process Are:
#1 Idealise.
#2 Visualise.
#3 Emotionalise.
#4 Verbalise.
#5 Materialise.

SUMMARY

Every creation and invention that we have and use today began with an idea in someone's mind.

We are living in today the results of what we created yesterday, and we will experience tomorrow the results of what we are creating today.

The boundaries of your life are not on the outside, the boundaries of your life are on the inside of you.

Your life will always move in the direction of your most dominant thoughts.

Imagination is everything. It is the preview of life's coming attractions.

Vision is powerful. When you habitually visualize it, you will materialize it, whatever *it* may be, good or bad.

Your subconscious mind has ways beyond your understanding to bring about whatever you plant within it, so be good to yourself and think magnificent thoughts.

When you start to be thankful and grateful in advance of the manifestation, this gets you in alignment for receiving.

When you and I want to create something in our world, our mouths will have to get involved.

You are not the victim, you are the creator.

CHAPTER 4

HOW TO INCREASE YOUR PERSONAL MAGNETISM TO ATTRACT SUCCESS

Personal magnetism is attractive. Whether it's a good sense of humour, or just a pleasing personality, we always admire those who have this positive personal magnetism. They seem to radiate confidence and easily draw others to themselves. They are the most successful leaders, the top sales people and the most popular at the office. This invisible quality within them works with a magnetic influence that attracts others to them as bees are attracted to honey. Ultimately, it's what's *in* them that is creating the power of attraction. This principle applies to everything in the universe. The ancient text says, "A man with many friends must show himself friendly." It is because he shows himself friendly that he attracts friends. This same law applies to success in every area of life, whether it is social success, leadership success, career success or financial success.

THE SECRETS OF NON VERBAL COMMUNICATION

People may or may not be able to know your thoughts, but they certainly can pick up your attitude. We do not need to be prophets or psychics in order to sense a person's attitude. In fact sometimes you would have to be blind *not* to see it, for our attitudes radiate from us through our facial expressions, our tone of voice and our body language. An individual's attitude can be seen and felt very quickly in every human interaction. Since you become what you think about most of the time, your attitude in any given situation will be the result of your state of mind toward that situation. That's how people can know pretty much what you are thinking, because they pick up your attitude.

They say that **much of our communication is non verbal**. What we are inwardly, we will express outwardly. If a person is angry, you sure can see it in their outward expression. If an individual is interested or uninterested they will let you know without even saying a word about it. We really don't hide as much from each other as we would like to think we do. People are far more intelligent than we usually give them credit for. If we want to have greater success in our relationships with other people, whether it is personal or professional, we can do so by understanding the principle of personal magnetism.

HOW TO CREATE A GOOD FIRST IMPRESSION

The first thing that people notice is your outward appearance. People are highly visual. The way you dress and groom yourself is an important factor of your personal magnetism. They say that when people view a property that's for sale, they make up their minds usually within the first few seconds of entering the door of the house. This can also be true when we meet new people as well. The way that we present ourselves outwardly says a lot about who we are inwardly. If you want to sell your house, do the best you can to clean it up, tidy it up and make it smell good. If you want to sell yourself to that company or that client, or even to that member of the opposite sex, you are going to have to present yourself the best you can. Most successful people usually present themselves clean and dressed appropriately for the occasion. They understand the importance of first impressions.

Some have the attitude, "Well, they can just take me or leave me." If you don't make the proper effort, they will most likely leave you.

TAKE A BRAND NEW LEASE ON LIFE

Have you ever noticed how divorce or widowhood ages some individuals, but not others? If the widow or divorcee feels that their life is over and that they have nothing left to live for, their inward thinking gives outward evidence. Others seem to manifest the very opposite. They spring to life with a new look, shed a few pounds or even a few stone. They take out a new gym membership, kit themselves out with a whole new wardrobe and then they show up looking like a brand new person. They are on a mission and they usually achieve it within a surprisingly short period of time. They refuse to give up on their dreams, and this kind of thinking gives them a brand new lease on life. Whether it's a new partner, a new career or business venture, **new thinking creates new opportunities**. We don't have to wait until we have hit rock bottom before we pick ourselves up. A decision to raise our thoughts to a higher level will affect our outward actions for the better, and better actions will create better results. All of this hinges on the way we think, and the state of our mind determines the state of our lives.

How to attract the opposite sex

The outward appearance is what creates the initial attraction. I learned this principle when I was at high school. I was attracted to the girls who were of a higher standard. They dressed nice and smelled good. Fortunately I was smart enough to realise that if I wanted a girlfriend of this standard, I was going to have to raise *my* standard to even get their attention. I was going to have to dress nice and smell good too. Some guys aren't smart enough to know that sweet smelling, sexy and gorgeous girls are not attracted to sweaty and unwashed stinky boys. This was a good lesson to learn at a reasonably young age, and it paid out high rewards for me in my youth in the form of nice girlfriends. This principle remains the same at every level and in every interaction. Those who are even outwardly dressed to a similar standard can spot each other across a crowded room. As the saying goes, "Birds of a feather flock together."

However there is **a deeper level of attraction** between humans where people who are like minded or we could say, are of **the same spirit**, tend to *gravitate* towards each other and feel comfortable together. We all feel far more comfortable associating with others who are just like us. Successful people can recognise other successful people from a distance. One woman said, "If only I could marry a rich man, then all my problems would be over." Another replied, "If you want to marry someone rich, be the kind of person someone rich would *want* to marry."

How You Can Become a Money Magnet

Prosperity flows to the individual who is in harmony with prosperity. When you are radiating a sense of failure and sending out vibes of poor me, this will not attract success and riches into your life. As you become more success minded, you will begin to attract more success. The more you think about your lack of success, the more you will repel success away from you. Feelings of lack will not attract abundance any more than a salesman without confidence or belief in himself and his products will attract an abundance of orders. You have to create you prosperity mentally first.

WEALTH AND SUCCESS VIBES

I heard of a successful business woman who while being interviewed was asked the question, "When you travel do you always go first class?" She replied, "**I always go first class, regardless of where I sit.**" She then went on to explain that going first class was an internal attitude. **Your internal beliefs and convictions are creating your external situations and circumstances.**

"As within, so without."
—The Emerald Tablet—

Regardless of your current financial situation, you can begin to feel wealthy right now, because compared with some people in the world today, you *are* wealthy. If you will **take your focus off of what you don't have, and begin to focus on what you do have**, you will begin to feel more positive about being wealthy immediately. This is the frequency you need to be on for wealth to be attracted to you. The old saying that, "Money goes to money" is true and this is one main reason why the rich get richer and the poor get poorer. "**Poor me vibes" attract more poverty, and wealthy vibes (wealthy thoughts**

and wealthy feelings) attract more wealth. When you are radiating I am so blessed vibes, you will attract back to you more blessing.

> "While it may seem that there are many roadblocks on your journey to wealth, the only real obstacle is what you believe, think, and feel about money."
> —Bob Proctor—

Greet money like it's a good friend, because it is. Money can be exchanged for lots of enjoyable things and pleasant experiences. Money can pay for your ticket to share in the good things that life has to offer. Don't call it dirty cash or filthy lucre. Respect it, appreciate it, be thankful for it and not only will money come to you, but it will stay with you. Money can't wait to get away from some people, they don't respect it enough and it doesn't hang around them for long, it gravitates towards those who will treat it like it deserves to be treated. **A change of attitude towards money will increase your personal magnetism to attract it.**

ATTITUDES, AFFIRMATIONS AND ACTIONS THAT ATTRACT SUCCESS

Every thought that you think and every word that you speak is a form of affirmation. When you affirm a thing, you are making it firm in *your* life. Much of our habitual thinking and speaking about money is very negative and often we don't even realise it. Most of our thoughts and words are about our struggle financially, our bills, our debts and the increasing costs of everything. This is only affirming our lack and insufficiency. **We have to get our minds and our mouths *off* of the**

things that we don't want, and begin thinking and talking about the things that we *do* want.

Our thoughts and words today are creating our tomorrow. You are a living magnet, and you will attract into your life that which is in harmony with your regular thought patterns.

One way to begin to shift your focus is to write out your goals for the future. There is something significant about writing out your goals on paper that is the first sign of them manifesting in the physical world. When you concentrate your thoughts, and write down what you desire your life to be like one year from now, you will be programming that instruction into your subconscious mind and it will begin to alert you to ideas, opportunities and actions you can take in order to bring it to pass.

> "There is the magnetised man who is full of confidence and faith. He knows that he is born to win and to succeed. Then there is the type of man who is demagnetised. He is full of fears and doubts.
> —Dr Joseph Murphy—

Whatever it is that you want to *win* in life you will first have to develop **the winning attitude** towards it. When you count your defeats you will reaffirm that failure feeling, but when you count your blessings and all that you have to be grateful for, you'll begin to stir up **that winning feeling**. A healthy confidence, backed by an unwavering persuasion that you are supposed to win in life, will produce the magnetism necessary to attract it. Fears and doubts will drain your spirit of the energy you need to succeed.

Associate with those who will feed your faith, and avoid those who feed your fears and your doubts. It was William Shakespeare who said, "Our doubts are traitors and make us lose the good we oft might win."

> "If you think you are beaten you are, if you think you dare not you don't. If you'd like to win, but you think you can't, it's almost certain you won't. If you think you'll lose, you've lost, for out in the world we find, success begins with a fellows will, it's all in the state of mind.
>
> If you think you're outclassed you are, you've got to think high to rise. You've got to be sure of yourself before you can ever win a prize. Life's battles don't always go to the stronger or faster man, but sooner or later the one who wins is the one who thinks he can."
>
> —Walter D. Wintle—

THE POWER OF A QUALITY DECISION

If you will think back to every goal you have ever achieved in your life this far, you will remember that before you achieved it, you made a decision to do so. Whether it was losing weight, passing your driving test or getting out of debt, once you get clear about what you want and make a quality decision that you are going to do it, there is a powerful energy released from within you and nothing will be able to stop you from achieving it.

Success is not an accident. Every person who has ever achieved anything significant, made a decision to do so. In reading the success stories of the wealthy, many were from backgrounds of poverty and they swore to themselves that they and their families would struggle no more, but somehow they would find a way to have and enjoy the good things that life has to offer. **This kind of decision has a power within**

it that should never be underestimated. When your goal becomes a burning desire within you, there is no time to be allowing your mind to dwell on the trivial things that would divert your attention away from your dream.

Napoleon Hill, in his book, "Think and Grow Rich" said, "There is one quality which one must possess to win, and that is definiteness of purpose, the knowledge of what one wants, and a burning desire to possess it."

This is the inner magnetism that attracts success. How strong or weak is your magnetic pull on success? The question to ask yourself is this, how bad do you want it? Whatever success means to you and in whatever area you want to achieve it, the principle is the same.

There are three levels of so called "wanting" that T Harv Eker mentions in his millionaire mind seminars.

The first level is, "I *want* to be rich."

You will probably have noticed that wanting doesn't necessarily always lead to having. Millions of people *want* to be rich, but relatively few of them are. This level of wanting is like *wishing* it would fall into your lap, like winning the lottery or being left a fortune by a rich relative that you didn't know that you had. This is a weak level of wanting and usually leads to more wanting.

Napoleon Hill said, "**There is a difference between wishing for a thing and being ready to receive it.**"

The second level of wanting is, "I *choose* to be rich."

Choosing is much stronger than mere wishing, it infers making a decision, which also reveals that you are accepting personal responsibility for where you currently are in life and that **you have within you the power to be able to do something about it.** T Harv Eker mentions that the word decision comes from the latin word decidere, which means to kill off any other alternatives. So choosing is much better than mere wishing. But there is still a higher level.

The third level of wanting is, "I *commit* to being rich."

Most of us are not fully committed to being rich and that's the real reason why we are not. Commitment is the highest level of wanting. It infers burning your bridges behind you. There is no way back to where you used to be. Personally, being honest I would have to say that I am not fully committed to being rich financially to the same degree that some others are, but **I am committed to financial freedom.** This can mean different things to different people. For me it means being without debt and having sufficient funds available to enjoy life and to be able to be a blessing to those I love. Thank God for those who are committed to being rich, most of them are helping to make our world a better place. Perhaps it's just that I don't personally have a big enough vision *yet*, because the bigger your vision, the more finance is required to fund it.

Money Can Bring Happiness

The mentality which says that money doesn't make you happy obviously doesn't have any plans to help anyone. You can do more good with money than you can do without it. When you are in a position financially to be able to do something good for someone and to see the joy in their faces as they receive it, certainly proves that **money can bring happiness after all.**

A few years ago I had my eye on a new television with a larger screen. When I began to think about what I would do with the one I currently had if I was going to purchase a new one, I thought of a girl I knew who was a single parent and had three young children. At that time I was aware that she only had a small portable TV. I offered her my TV and video recorder and she was happy to receive it. When I took it round and set it up, her children were all excited and happy with what they were receiving. I think I was almost as thrilled with giving away my old TV as I was with getting my new one.

This is just a small example of how being in a position financially to be able to give to others can bring much happiness to you. Once again, **whoever says that money doesn't make you happy doesn't have any plans to do good for anyone.** When you are not even in a position to be able to provide for and be generous to the most important people in your life, this doesn't bring you or anyone else happiness. To be able to see your own loved ones enjoying something nice is surely the least we should be aiming for.

Whatever your goals and dreams are, be it financial, physical, relational, spiritual or vocational, merely *wanting* them is probably not strong enough to make them happen. *Choose* to have your dream become a reality, and *commit* to seeing it fulfilled. **A burning desire within you for achieving your goal is the level of magnetism you'll need to pull it toward you and to *move you* toward it.** Are you willing to pay the price in order to have it? If you are, then no obstacle will be able to stand in your way, and you will become unstoppable.

SUMMARY

Our attitudes radiate from us through our facial expressions, our tone of voice and our body language.

Your attitude in any given situation will be the result of your state of mind toward that situation.

The first thing that people notice about you is your outward appearance. People are highly visual.

The way that we present ourselves outwardly says a lot about who we are inwardly.

If you want to marry someone rich, be the kind of person someone rich would want to marry.

When you are radiating a sense of failure and sending out vibes of poor me, this will not attract success and riches into your life. As you become more success minded, you will begin to attract more success.

Poor me vibes attract more poverty and wealthy vibes attract more wealth.

A change of attitude towards money will increase your personal magnetism to attract it

Once you get clear about what you want and make a quality decision that you are going to do it, there is a powerful energy released from within you and nothing will be able to stop you from achieving it.

CHAPTER 5

FAITH AND THE LAW OF ATTRACTION

"According to your faith be it unto you."
—Matthew 9:29—

THE POWER OF BELIEF

It is not my intention in this chapter to do an exhaustive study about religion, but rather to discuss the power of belief within *every* human being, (religious or non-religious) and the effects that those beliefs have on the results in our lives. It is also my intention to show that **the principles of the law of attraction** are all over the ancient scriptures and have indeed been around for thousands of years. It is also necessary to point out that our concept of God has a significant influence on many of our beliefs about life. **These ancient universal laws were established by the creator of the universe.** They are every bit as powerful today as they have ever been, and the world is waking up to the revelation of them. Many people are desperate for improvement in their lives and that's a great place to be. You will never change what you are prepared to tolerate, but discontentment is actually a creative state. As Bob Proctor says, "life can be absolutely phenomenal, and it should be, and it will be, when you start using the secret." And the secret is **the law of attraction**.

There have been many books written since the early 1900s on the subject of the law of attraction. One thing I've discovered is that you have to learn to filter everything you read and hear taught. I don't know of anyone who has arrived at perfection, and never changes their mind about anything to any degree over the years. As we all grow in knowledge and understanding, our perspective can change dramatically.

Much of the foundation that "The Secret" was built upon was written in the Bible thousands of years ago. Step one: Ask. Step two: Believe and Step three: Receive. Today many people can testify to having their prayers answered on certain occasions, yet also acknowledge that they have had prayers that seemed to go unanswered as well. This doesn't need to remain a mystery. I personally don't believe the problem lies on the sending end, but rather on the *receiving* end.

"God being a just power will always give you exactly what you have asked for.

But always bear in mind it is your innermost thoughts and images you are requesting, not the words to which you might only be paying lip service."

—Bob Proctor—

This can perhaps help explain one good reason why some prayers from good people *seem* to go unanswered. We have thought that all we had to do was say the prayer, and then wait for God to send the answer, not realising that **heaven can only do *for* you, what it can do *through* you**. It's so sad to see people who have become bitter against God, thinking that He didn't answer them when they prayed. We have to understand the part that *we* have to play in **receiving.**

If the doctor has told you that you only have six months to live, sometimes the worst thing you can do is ask the local church to pray about it, because they can have you dead in just six weeks. After prayer time, they'll be talking together saying, "Awe, it's such a shame, that poor woman, going to leave behind a young family, it's just terrible." Then after the funeral they'll talk about how it must not be God's will to heal everyone. Now I'm not suggesting that every church is like this, but some of us unfortunately can relate to this example.

I know of one well known minister who was told he had cancer, he deliberately didn't even tell his congregation, but only his wife. He said, "I know what to do." He got together his best books on the subject of divine healing. (Not the ones that tell you that it might *not* be God's will to heal everyone.) He got his bible and read through all the healing scriptures, he would meditate on them and believe he had received perfect health from the top of his head to the soles of his feet. He would give thanks and feel so grateful for good health and long life, until this image became more real to him than the doctor's report. After all sometimes the medical profession can even get it wrong. The next time he went for a scan, they couldn't find any trace of the cancer. He only told his congregation afterward as a testimony.

Wallace Wattles in 1910 wrote, "In the field of religion, the world cries out for the clergyman who can teach his hearers the true science of abundant life. He who teaches these details from the pulpit will never lack for a congregation. This is the gospel that the world needs, it will give increase of life, and men will hear it gladly, and will give liberal support to the man who brings it to them."

THE ANCIENT SCRIPTURES AND THE LAW OF ATTRACTION

Your *mind* is the bridge between the spirit realm and the physical realm. You *are* a spirit being, you *have* a soul (mind, will and emotions) and you *live* in a physical body. Standing between two realms, the realm of the spirit and the realm of the physical, is your mind. Once again, heaven cannot do anything *for* you that it cannot do *through* you. The mind bridge is often in need of renewal. If the bridge is out of order and closed, then nothing can pass through from the spirit to the physical. Your mind is the connecting link between the unformed and the formed worlds.

Some people's minds are closed to the subject under discussion, and if the *mind* bridge is closed, then it's very unlikely that there will be any deliveries show up in the physical realm. **Your mind has to be open to it, in order for it to show up in your life.** Open your mind to receive health, wealth and happiness, build the image of it within you. Whatever your mind is open to conceive and believe, you can potentially receive. Credit where it is due, with regards to **the process of believing and receiving**, the law of attraction explains this more clearly than I've ever heard it before.

"For the thing I greatly feared has come upon me, and
what I dreaded has happened to me."
—Job 3:25—

It is of significance that the expression "greatly feared" is used. This was not simply a passing fearful thought. This was a regularly visited pattern of habitual thinking. Fortunately it has been scientifically proven that **a positive thought is many times more powerful than a negative thought**. However if we persist in thinking fearful thoughts like Job did, we will create a gap in our hedge of protection through which undesirable things can reach us. **This universal law has been operational for thousands of years**.

Faith and fear are both spiritual forces and have attractive power within them. Fear seems to be contagious. If you are hanging around others who have it you are likely to catch it yourself. Spirit is transferable, whether it's good or bad. Discouragement and hopelessness can spread like a virus. The standards of those that we associate with regularly tend to become our own.

SPIRITUAL AND MENTAL ATMOSPHERES

We are all subject to many thoughts throughout each day and much of these are not our own but are picked up from other individuals and even from the general mentality of the environment that we are in at the time. It takes a person of strong character and self control to be in a negative environment for long periods of time and not be affected by the general mentality that makes up the atmosphere in that location or situation. Every gathering of people has an atmosphere, whether it's a church, a football match or the local bars and restaurants. Even towns and cities, and certain areas within the town or city will each have a different kind of atmosphere. This is determined largely by the collective mentality of the individuals in that location. **Being surrounded by success minded people who have good values and a positive outlook is a valuable place to be.** Even if your own current surroundings are not ideal, you can take charge of your own immediate space and control your *personal* vibration. Remember you too are contributing to the atmosphere everywhere you go, your thoughts and feelings are adding to the situation and making it either better or worse.

"All the days of the desponding and afflicted are made evil
by anxious thoughts and forebodings, but he who has a glad
heart has a continual feast regardless of circumstances."
—Proverbs 15:15. The amplified Bible—

Worry and anxiety are forms of fear. Anxious thoughts will create
the circumstances and situations that you are worrying about. The
Oxford dictionary defines foreboding as, "Feeling that trouble is
coming." Two major points revealed in this text are firstly, that a life
filled with despondency and affliction is called evil (not good,) and also
that it is *made* that way by the individual's thoughts and feelings, (not
by fate or bad luck.) This doesn't infer that the *individual* is a bad or
evil person, but that the conditions being produced are. The wonderful
truth that sets us free is that we can begin to create and produce new
and better outward conditions by winning the battle in the arena of
the mind.

The law of attraction also says that our thoughts which are
accompanied by strong emotional feelings and beliefs will attract things
faster into our lives, than thoughts that have little or no feeling attached
to them. The latter part of the text sounds like a much better place to
live, for he who has a glad or happy heart will enjoy a continual feast,
regardless of circumstances.

"Mind is the master power that molds and makes, and
man is mind, and evermore he takes the tool of thought,
and shaping what he wills, brings forth a thousand joys or
a thousand ills.

We think in secret and it comes to pass, our world is but
our looking glass."
—James Allen. Author of: As a man thinketh.—

The human will is involved. Man has been given the right to a free will and even his creator will not override his choices, so it is in his own interest to take and use his God given mental faculties and create a thousand joys, not a thousand ills. Just as many crimes and evil acts of people are pre-meditated, so also the great achievements that bless and enrich many people's lives begin in the arena of the mind. **Where the mind goes, the man usually follows**.

How Your Beliefs Create Your Reality

"We've known in the healing arts of a placebo effect. A placebo is something that supposedly has no impact and no effect on the body, like a sugar pill. You tell the patient that this is just as effective, and what happens is the placebo sometimes has the same effect, if not greater effect, than the medication that is supposed to be designed for that effect. They have found out that the human mind is the biggest factor in the healing arts, sometimes more so than the medication."

—Dr John Demartini—

I heard Bishop John Francis from London England tell about a man who had been in hospital for some tests and the doctor got his test results mixed up with another patient with the same surname. When the doctor read the results to him he said, "But I feel fine." The doctor explained all the symptoms that would soon begin to show up in his body according to the test results. The man started going downhill from that day onward and all the symptoms that the doctor mentioned were beginning to manifest, he ended up hospitalised and dying. When it was discovered that there had been a mistake and the doctor very humbly told him so, the man said, "What! You mean there is nothing wrong with me? I'm not going to die after all? It wasn't long before he walked out of the hospital and went back home well.

Yes, there is real illness and suffering out there. However there is a lot of suffering in many lives, be it physical, mental or even financial that we bring into our own lives and keep in our lives because of our subconscious beliefs and negative expectations. The law of belief says that whatever *you* believe with conviction becomes *your* reality.

THE SHIELD OF FAITH

"Above all, taking the shield of faith with which you will be able to quench all the fiery darts of the wicked one."
—Ephesians 6:16—

Faith here is described as a shield of protection. Faith is a shield that cannot be penetrated by *any* evil thing. The flip side of the force of attraction is the power to repel. We repel away from us anything that is not in harmony with us. In the movie "300", starring Gerard Butler, the shields his men carried into battle went right around their bodies and protected them front and back.

I heard a statement from Charles Capps, a minister in the word of faith, about this verse. He said, **"The shield of faith is created around us by the faith filled words we speak, it's like a spiritual aura that surrounds us as we walk."** Think about that. Each one of us is radiating out from ourselves vibrations according to the thoughts we are thinking and the words we have been speaking. If our thoughts and words are full of faith, we are taking up the shield of faith and no weapon formed against us shall be able to prosper. In Psalm 92, David said, "No evil shall befall me, nor shall any plague or calamity come near my dwelling." Now that's a faith man talking. True faith gives off positive vibrations and attracts back that which is on the same frequency. Fear likewise will attract to itself according to its own kind.

THE VISION OF FAITH

True faith has a vision. Faith sees the answer before the natural eye can see it. Faith gets happy in advance of the manifestation in the material world. See yourself *being* the kind of person you desire to be. See yourself *doing* the kind of things you desire to do. And see yourself *having* the kind of things you desire to have. If you just can't see yourself living in a nice house, in good health, debt free and enjoying abundant life, then it's very unlikely that you ever will.

> "The law of attraction simply states that like attracts like. The more you create the vibration—the mental and emotional states—of already having something, the faster you attract it to you.
>
> This is an immutable law of the universe and critical to accelerating your rate of success."
> —Jack Canfield. Author of: The Success Principles.—

THE POWER OF FAITH FILLED WORDS.

True faith has a confession. Faith calls those things that be not as though they were. That's how they come into being. If you prefer to call it like it is, you'll simply get more of things just like it is. God looked into the darkness in Genesis chapter 1 and said, "Let there be light." Though the external situation was very dull and dark, God had light within himself and he spoke it out.

The universal law of attraction doesn't simply respond to words by themselves, it responds more to how you and I *feel* about the words we use. It is our inner feelings that are giving off the vibes that attract according to their kind. This is one reason why positive confessions and affirmations do not always work for everyone. It is not the words themselves that produce results. It is the spirit you fill those words with. Faith filled words contain creative spiritual substance.

FAITH IN ACTION

True faith has action. Faith without works is dead. **Act as if** it's already yours, and take steps toward the direction of your goals. You'll be attracted to things and things will be attracted to you. If you habitually think success thoughts, your life has got no choice but to become it. If you can go there in the mind, you can go there in the body. Your body will obey you, whatever you decide on and make up your mind to do, though the body may resist at first because of past habit patterns, it will eventually obey your instruction. Your mind is the control centre and your body will react to your habitual thoughts. When you habitually think on the other side of the boundary line, your body will begin to go in that direction. **It's what's on the inside of us that really controls our lives, not the circumstances outside us.** You can change your spiritual aura (your magnetic field) by changing your thoughts and feelings. When you are thinking it and feeling it in your soul, you are on course to becoming it.

THE ATTRACTOR FACTOR

We don't always attract what we want, we attract according to what we are. There is an old saying that, **"We are *where* we are because we** are *what* we are, and we are *what* we are because of our habitual thinking." It is not the outward front we may put on for others to see, but what we really think deep within ourselves that determines what we will attract back to us. Whatever it is that you are habitually thinking and feeling is the blueprint for what is in the process of coming back to you, because like attracts like. You can't be constantly offering feelings of self pity and unhappiness and then attract back to you situations that fill you with joy. **Send out some joy and it will come back to you multiplied**. If the farmer wants to change the kind of harvest he is reaping, he simply has to change the kind of seed he is sowing. As Rhonda Byrne says it, "**Life is not happening to you, life is *responding* to you**." The boomerang principle states that *whatever* you send out is what will come back to you.

Accepting this principle can move you into the proactive driver's seat in life, instead of being a passive passenger ending up at destinations of someone else's choosing. It is a passive attitude of irresponsibility when one thinks that life is just *happening* to them. But to realise and accept that life is actually *responding* to you puts power and authority to create your own future back into your own hands where it belongs. **Man has been given far more authority in the earth realm than he realises**. Something within the heart of man leaps when the truth about who he really is begins to be revealed. The sleeping giant within begins to awaken. Thomas Edison wrote, "If we did all the things we are capable of doing, we would literally astonish ourselves."

THE PROSPEROUS SOUL

"Beloved I wish above all things that you may prosper
and be in health, even as your soul prospers."

—3 John: 2—

The heart of man is the centre of his being. The Apostle Paul referred to this as the inward man. The Apostle Peter called him the hidden man of the heart. Whatever name you call it, your inner being has to be in health and prosper, if your outer life is ever going to be healthy and prosperous. Without a prosperous soul, you cannot prosper outwardly. You will prosper and be in health *as* your soul prospers. Your mind, your emotions and your will are all involved in believing and receiving. This is both a spiritual and a psychological truth. A change of heart brings a change of life.

"A man of perverse heart does not prosper."
—Proverbs 17:20—

God is not the one keeping prosperity from him. His own heart (thinking) is keeping prosperity from him. It surely is *perverse* thinking to believe that the rich, loving father God would will that his own children struggle in poverty and somehow He is getting glory from all this. Being poor does not equal being spiritual. Many religious interpretations of scripture have robbed us of the good life, and if we continue to hold onto those beliefs and erroneous superstitions they will continue to rob us. One meaning of the word perverse is twisted. And twisted thinking concerning the will and the plan of God will repel prosperity away from us. Our concept of God should be that He loves us and is for us, not against us.

"Be ye transformed, by the renewing of your mind."
—Romans 12:2—

Transformation in a person's life is a *result* of the renewing of the mind. If we really want to help people change their lives for the better, we will have to help them to change the way they think. A drug addict will remain a drug addict until they change the way they think, a poor person will stay poor until they get rid of the poverty mindset. It has often been said, "Give a man a fish and you'll feed him for a day, teach him how to fish and you'll feed him for a lifetime." Lasting change only happens when a person changes on the inside. When knowledge gets down on the inside of you and becomes a part of you, when your deep rooted beliefs truly become positive your whole world is about to change for the better.

"Do not curse the King, even in your thought, do not curse the rich, even in your bedroom, for a bird of the air may carry your voice, and a bird in flight may tell the matter."
—Ecclesiastes 10:20—

The text here shows not only to guard what you say, but that even our *thoughts* have a way of being carried and what we think can somehow come back to us. Whenever we criticise or condemn the rich and successful, we are repelling success and riches away from ourselves. You cannot attract what you are condemning as being wrong.

"Now acquaint yourself with Him, and be at peace; thereby good will come to you."
—Job 22:21—

Getting acquainted with the *true* character and personality of God will create a wonderful peace within us. And this peace within us will *cause* good to come into our lives. Seeking the Kingdom and His righteousness will cause all these good things to be added to us.

Seeking religion doesn't seem to do it. There is a big difference between righteousness and religiousness.

THE PERSON AND THE PRINCIPLES

The scriptures reveal both the *person* of God, and the *principles* of God. As Dr Mike Murdock says, "One is the King and the other is the kingdom. One is the Son of God and the other is the system of God. One is an experience *with* God and the other is the expertise *of* God. His person creates your peace and His principles create your prosperity." Let us get to know both the person and the principles.

> "This book of the law shall not depart from your mouth, but you shall meditate in it day and night, that you may observe to do according to all that is written in it, for then you will make your way prosperous, and then you will have good success."
> —Joshua 1:8—

Think, speak and act according to the good word written, and *you* will *make* your way prosperous. *Think and grow rich.* There is nothing new about meditation. Joshua tapped into Divine wisdom through meditation, and he and all the Israelites entered into the promised land flowing with milk and honey, where they prospered and had good success. Things get down on the inside of you when you meditate on them. Repetition is one of the most effective ways of learning. You can know it in your head and it won't do you much good, but when it gets down into your heart and takes root within you, your life will never be the same again.

SUMMARY

Faith and fear are both spiritual forces and have attractive power within them.

Where the mind goes, the man follows.

What you believe with conviction becomes your reality.

The shield of faith cannot be penetrated by any evil thing.

True faith gives off positive vibrations and attracts back that which is on the same frequency.

Faith has a vision, faith has a confession and faith has actions.

Lasting change can only happen when a person changes on the inside.

Whenever we criticise or condemn the rich and successful, we are repelling success and riches away from ourselves. You cannot attract what you are condemning as being wrong.

Wealth must be conceived on the inside before it can be received on the outside.

Life is not happening to you, life is responding to you.

Chapter 6

The Advanced Laws of Prosperity

Advanced means higher than or beyond the normal. These advanced laws are not for the faint hearted. They are spiritual laws that will unleash a supernatural empowerment into your total life prosperity. Supernatural here refers to that which is above and beyond the natural. Natural progress is good, but supernatural progress is even better. The release of the supernatural through your cooperation with these advanced laws of prosperity will accelerate your success more than you could have ever imagined possible.

Faith and Financial Freedom

"If you have been brought up to believe that being wealthy is not spiritual, then I highly recommend that you read the millionaires of the bible series by Catherine Ponder.

In these glorious books you will discover that Abraham, Isaac, Jacob, Joseph, Moses and Jesus were not only prosperity teachers, but also millionaires themselves."

—Rhonda Byrne. Author of: The Secret.—

At Rhonda's recommendation I began to read the books of Catherine Ponder. These have been extremely helpful to me personally and have inspired my own further personal study of the scriptures in this area. I have found both from personal experience and from conversation with many others that one of the main *subconscious* hindrances to financial success has been past religious interpretations of scripture that have condemned and disapproved of it. Therefore it is vital that we understand and believe that God is not against our success financially, but that the scriptures repeatedly show that wherever God commands His blessing, wealth and prosperity have a habit of showing up. If you have any struggle from a religious point of view over whether or not it's ok to desire to prosper financially, highlight and read often the bible quotations throughout this book.

BREAKING THE BARRIERS TO YOUR WEALTHY PLACE

Some of the barriers to our wealthy place simply have to be broken practically. Others have to be broken mentally. However there are also barriers that are spiritual in nature, and no matter how much we do practically towards our freedom, it always seems so hard to ever get ahead. **There is a power that you are about to discover and when it is activated in your life, it will be as though you are being assisted by unseen forces, and indeed you are.** Spiritual barriers must be broken by spiritual power.

> "Thus says the Lord to his anointed . . . I will go before you and make the crooked places straight. I will break in pieces the gates of bronze, and cut the bars of iron. I will give you the treasures of darkness and hidden riches of secret places. That you may know that I, the Lord, who call you by your name, am the God of Israel."
>
> —The Prophet Isaiah. Chapter 45:1-3 NKJV—

Gates and bars are constructed with the intention of keeping you out of the territory, and to stop you from entering into it. There are barriers between you and your wealthy place, and they will keep you out of it for the rest of your life, *unless* these barriers are broken. The text above reveals that **there are hidden riches in secret places**. It also reveals that God is not the one who is keeping you from reaching them. On the contrary, He is willing to release His power to break in pieces every barrier that may stand in your way, if only you will give Him permission to get involved. There is supernatural assistance available for our advancement and progress in life. Poverty is not simply a physical condition. Poverty is a mentality. There is a difference between being broke and being poor. Someone said, "I may be broke, but I'm not poor." Being broke is a temporary situation, being poor is a mentality.

> "Now to Him who is able to do exceedingly abundantly above all that we ask or think, according to the power that works in us."
>
> —Ephesians 3:20 NKJV—

He is able to do much *more* than we can imagine, but He doesn't do it without our involvement. He can only do *for* us according to the measure of the power that works *within* us. **We do not receive**

according to what God is *able* to do, we receive according to *our* faith. As *you* have believed, it will be done for you. This is how the kingdom works. **Everything in the kingdom works by faith, and nothing in the kingdom works without faith**. All things are possible, for them that believe.

> "For indeed the gospel was preached to us as well as to
> them, but the word which they heard did not profit them,
> not being mixed with faith in those who heard it."
> —Hebrews 4:2 NKJV—

Every word from God has to be mixed with faith in order for it to profit or benefit the hearers. The word of God is likened unto seed. A seed will bring forth a miracle only when it is planted in good soil and watered. The word of God contains salvation seed, healing seed, victory and prosperity seed. **Whatever kind of harvest you are in need of, go and find the appropriate kind of seed. Plant the seed on the inside of you, feed it and water it and the harvest will show up in your life.** Meditate on the word of God's supernatural barrier breaking power, until you catch the spirit of the barrier breaker.

Activating spiritual assistance by faith can accelerate your progress far beyond your natural ability would ever be able to achieve in the same period of time.

One day of favour is worth a thousand days of labour. Divine favour can have you at the right places, at the right times. With supernatural assistance change can happen quickly, even overnight.

THE DIVINE PLAN FOR YOUR SUCCESS

"For I know the plans I have for you declares the Lord,
plans to prosper you and not to harm you, plans to give you
hope and a future."
—Jeremiah 29:11 NIV—

There is a Divine plan for your success. If you have read much at all in the way of self help material, you will know the importance of having specific goals and definite plans to reach them. For many years I didn't quite know what I really wanted to do, so I pretty much took whatever opportunities came along. Even while being in this place, it was comforting to know that there was a Divine plan for me that included prosperity and hope for the future. The more I began to learn about how to tap into Divine wisdom and grow in understanding of life principles and universal laws, the more I began to live a purpose driven life.

THE POWER OF THE BLESSING

Have you ever heard the saying that **a Jew can make more money accidentally, than a gentile can make on purpose?** You will never convince a Jew that it is God's will for them to be poor. They know their covenant too well to let any western religion talk them out of it. It would serve the rest of us well to take a leaf out of their book and refuse to let religion talk us out of our heritage either. It is interesting that everyone seems to want to claim Abraham as their father. The Arabs, the Jews and the Christians all claim that *they* are the seed of Abraham.

Abraham was a blessed man. Genesis chapter thirteen and verse two tells us that he was *very* rich in livestock, in silver and in gold. In chapter twenty four and verse one we read that the Lord had blessed Abraham in all things. King Solomon later wrote in the book of proverbs, chapter ten and verse twenty two that, "**The blessing of the Lord makes rich, and He adds no sorrow with it**." King David wrote in the book of Psalms one hundred and twelve and verse three that, wealth and riches would be in the house of the blessed man. The apostle Paul in the book of Galatians chapter three and verse sixteen writes, now to Abraham *and his seed* were the promises made. No wonder everyone wants to claim Abraham as their father, for **this blessing has a pattern throughout scripture of producing wealth and prosperity in the lives of those who have it.**

Abraham had two sons, Ishmael and Isaac. They say that the Arabs are descendants of Ishmael and that the Jews are descendents of Isaac. So as the seed of Abraham from a natural point of view, there is an inheritance of blessing available for them all. We read concerning Isaac in Genesis chapter twenty six and verses twelve through to fourteen that, "Isaac sowed in that land, and reaped in the same year a hundredfold, and the Lord blessed him. The man began to prosper, and continued prospering until he became very prosperous, for he had possessions of flocks and possessions of herds and a great number of servants. So the Philistines envied him."

This blessing seemed to be passed down from generation to generation and it always seemed to produce prosperity in the lives of those who received it. Isaac had two sons, Jacob and Esau. We read that Jacob valued this blessing more than Esau did and he ended up being the one who received the greater portion of it. In Genesis chapter thirty and verse forty three we read that Jacob became exceedingly prosperous, and had large flocks, female and male servants, and camels and donkeys.

In each case, the *blessing* was responsible for their prosperity. **The word "Blessing" in the dictionary is defined as, invoking divine favour and conferring well being or prosperity.** The blessing was passed on to the next generation usually by words spoken over them, and most importantly it was *received* by belief in the power of the words that were spoken.

Faith in the promise given was and still is the force that attracts the blessing. It doesn't happen automatically, but it is *activated* by faith. Once again the Apostle Paul wrote in Galatians chapter three, verse nine. "So those who have *faith* are *blessed* along with Abraham, the man of faith." Now stay with me, for there is some *really* good news. In verse eight, the scripture says that God preached the gospel in advance to Abraham saying, "All nations will be *blessed* through you."

Everyone is claiming Abraham as their father and so they should be, for the gospel is that **all nations** can receive this *blessing* by faith. Every group likes to think that they are the special ones, and no one else is as special as us. The truth is that we are *all* special and the promise is unto *all* them that *believe*. **It was and is the plan of God that all nations and every family on the earth be blessed.** There is more than enough blessing for everyone, and there is no need to fight each other over it. In fact when we start to fight each other, we cut ourselves off from it. Religious bitterness and hatred will not attract blessing, on the contrary it will repel it away from us. God is no respecter of persons and neither are the universal laws that He has set in motion. We can all find financial freedom through faith in the blessing, and by understanding the law of attraction.

THE PROSPERITY GOSPEL

The term "Prosperity gospel" is a label that has been given to those who believe that God's blessing in the financial and material arena is not reserved *only* for when we all get to heaven, but is also available right here and now in this life. Some shudder at the thought and have vehemently opposed such a message. Now for sure the gospel includes much more than financial matters, but it's interesting that in the above quoted New Testament scripture, where *God Himself* preached the gospel in advance to Abraham, He talked about **the blessing.** And in Abraham's experience, this blessing included material prosperity. God also told him that it was not *only* for Abraham himself, but unto *all* the families on the earth. The third chapter in Galatians, verses thirteen and fourteen tell us that the very reason Jesus died on the cross was to redeem us from the curse, so that *the blessing of Abraham* might come upon the gentiles in and through Him. Think about that.

The blessing and the curse is listed in the book of Deuteronomy chapter twenty eight. And you will find that poverty is listed under the curse, and prosperity is listed under the blessing. **How in the world did religion manage to convince us that being broke was spiritual and being rich was sinful.** This is the very *opposite* from what the scriptures say. Now greed and selfishness are still bad attitudes, but you will find that those attitudes can be found in those who lack money just as much if not even more, than they are found in those who have plenty of it. Some people both religious and non religious, will try to make you feel guilty about even desiring more money, as if there is something wrong with that desire. One thing that they all seem to have in common is that they are all broke, and if you take on their opinions as your own, you will become just like them.

THE ANCIENT LAW OF PROSPERITY

Catherine Ponder in her classic book, "The Dynamic Laws of Prosperity," devotes an entire chapter to the ancient law of prosperity. This was a practice observed in honour to God, whom they considered to be the source of all blessing. In the Old Testament book of the prophet Malachi, God made promises to those who would bring a tithe of their increase as an offering into His house.

> "Try me now in this, says the Lord of hosts. and see if I will not open for you the windows of heaven.
>
> And pour you out a blessing that there will not be room enough to receive it.
>
> And I will rebuke the devourer for your sakes, so that he will not destroy the fruit of your ground.
>
> Nor shall the vine fail to bear fruit for you in the field, says the Lord of hosts. And all nations will call you blessed, for you will be a delightful land, says the Lord of hosts."
>
> —Malachi 3:10—

I was fortunate from my late teens on through to my early thirties to be involved in a Church that taught and believed these principles. I guess every Church believes you should tithe, but their emphasis is more often on how it will benefit the Church and its needs, instead of on how it will prosper the tither. In this setting it is understandable why many are hesitant to part with the tithe. The scripture clearly says that it is the individual who will be blessed, protected and prospered through tithing. It isn't just the act of giving that releases the blessing, but it is the faith and expectation of God keeping His word, and doing what He said He would do, that brings into manifestation that which has been promised.

THE POWER OF AGREEMENT

I believe that there has to be agreement between the giver and the receiver concerning what the outcome is going to be as the result of the financial seed sown. Many have the so called humble attitude that, well I don't give expecting anything back in return. While its appropriate not to expect anything back from the individual or the specific organisation that you are giving to. It is unscriptural not to expect anything back from God as a result of giving as He directs. The apostle Paul gave insight into this in the New Testament.

> "But this I say, he who sows sparingly will also reap sparingly, and he who sows bountifully will also reap bountifully."
> "So let each one give as he purposes in his heart, not grudgingly or of necessity, for God loves a cheerful giver."
> "And God is able to make all grace abound toward you, that you always having all sufficiency in all things, may have an abundance for every good work."
> —2 Corinthians 9:6-8—

It is important to note that the context of this text is financial. Money given in an offering is likened to seed sown. And the apostle Paul released his faith in agreement with the givers faith for a *multiplied* return on their offering.

"Now may He who supplies seed to the sower, and
bread for food, supply and multiply the seed you have sown
and increase the fruits of your righteousness."
—2 Corinthians 9:10—

Not everyone will dare to pray like this over your offering. They may pray that the money in the offering will be multiplied for the needs of the Church to be met. But that's not what the apostle Paul prayed for. He prayed that the giver would receive back a multiplication of the financial seed sown.

To continue with the analogy used of sowing and reaping, there is a great illustration in the parable of the sower told in the book of Matthew chapter thirteen. The only seed that produced a harvest was the seed that was sown into *good* ground. It yielded a crop of up to a hundredfold. Seventy five percent of the seed sown did not bring back *any* return. I believe that we ought to check out the soil that we are sowing into, to make sure that it is good ground. There are a couple of things to look for. First of all, what are they doing with the offering you are sending? Are they managing the money well, or are they mismanaging it? Secondly and most importantly with regards to your potential harvest or lack of it, are they in agreement with you and believing together with you for a multiplication of your seed sown?

"Again I say to you that if two of you agree on earth
concerning anything that they ask, it will be done for them
by my Father in heaven."
—Matthew 18:19—

If one party is thinking and believing one thing, and the other party is thinking and believing something else, then there is no agreement. This applies with regard to *whatever* it is you are asking for in prayer, from physical healing to financial increase. There is power in agreement.

THE LAW OF GIVING AND RECEIVING

Giving is certainly not limited to money that you place in an offering, or send as a gift to a ministry or charity. **When we give to life our best, life will give to us its best**. The entire principle of business is based on giving and receiving. In order to increase your receiving, you just have to increase your giving. Any company that will increase the quality and the quantity of its products and services will receive an increase of customers and ultimately an increase in profits.

> "Give and it will be given to you:
> Good measure, pressed down, shaken together, and running over will be put into your bosom.
> For with the same measure that you use, it will be measured back to you."
> —Luke 6:38—

When we give, we should do so with an expectation of increase in return, just as the farmer sows seed into the field expecting a harvest. It would be foolishness for the farmer to plant seed and yet have no expectation of it coming back to him multiplied. This would also be a violation of the laws of this universe. Our world began with an abundant creation, and *everything* begins with a seed. Every seed contains within it the potential of multiplication. You yourself are walking evidence of the law of seedtime and harvest. The billions of people alive on the planet today are evidence that sowing seed produces a harvest.

> "While the earth remains, seedtime and harvest shall
> not cease."
> —Genesis 8:22—

There are a multitude of different types of seeds. Friendship is a seed, kindness is a seed. Encouragement is a seed. Cheating and stealing from others are seeds. Your thoughts and your words are seeds. Whatever kind of seed you are sowing will come back to you multiplied. **Harvest never just shows up, it is always a result of seedtime.** Giving nothing will simply bring back a harvest of nothing. If you are blessed it didn't just happen. If you are cursed it didn't just happen. Whatever kind of harvest is manifesting in your life right now, there was at sometime a seed or seeds sown that have *caused* the results you are now experiencing. Good health is a result and poor health is also a result. Your current weight is a result, and your financial net worth is a result.

> "A man's harvest in life is based solely on the seeds that
> he has sown in his past."
> —Galatians 6:7. Philips Translation—

Giving is not a gamble. According to the unbreakable and inescapable laws of life, *whatever* you give out will provoke a response. Gratitude for what you have is the seed for more. Lack of gratitude for what you have can even cause you to lose it. Your future harvests will be the result of the new seeds that you begin to sow from this day forward. When you activate these advanced laws of prosperity, your increase is divinely guaranteed. Your future will be whatever you choose it to be. Our choice of seed and the exercise of the discipline necessary in sowing it is the determining factor in what our tomorrow will look like. **Every belief and every action we take is a choice, just as every disbelief**

and inaction is also a choice. It takes *faith* to invoke supernatural blessing, the rewards are reserved for *them* that *believe*.

The Secret Combination

Life can be likened to a combination lock, and if can you enter the correct numbers in the correct order, the lock will open for you. And **when the lock opens for you, you immediately have access to all the good that life has to offer.** This book contains a unique combination of self help and spiritual help principles. And I believe that this combination is necessary to enter into full abundant life success.

We have *our* part to play and God has His part to play. We cannot do God's part for Him and He will not do our part for us. Self help teaching will educate us concerning what our part is and what *we* must do in order to help ourselves. Spiritual teaching instructs us in the knowledge of the supernatural assistance available to us through *faith*. It is not all one and none of the other that brings wholeness to us, but a combination of the two. When we are doing our part and God is doing His part, success is inevitable. Partnership with another can help both parties to achieve greater results than either one would ever be able to accomplish on their own. And this partnership between God and man is extremely powerful.

Self Help and Spiritual Help

I believe in self help and I also believe in God's help, and I study and teach both. If you are not willing to do something to help yourself, why should you expect God to do something to help you? **A miracle can get you out of immediate trouble, but ignorance will simply recreate your crisis.** It's lack of knowledge that causes people to perish. Often we are waiting on God to move, when He is waiting on us to move. It's like a game of chess. God will always move when it's His turn, but He will never move when it's *our* turn. When we make our move, God will be faithful to make His move. Self help informs us of what we can do to help ourselves. It instructs us to focus on what we have been given to work with. This is in agreement with universal spiritual principles.

"It is easy to understand that the nearer we live to the source of wealth, the more wealth we shall receive.

The soul that is always grateful lives in closer touch with God than the one which never looks to Him in thankful acknowledgement."

—Wallace D Wattles—

It can be quite off putting when people go to the extreme of not being able to acknowledge their *own* part in their success. This extreme says, "God did it" to everything. The other extreme is also incorrect if we refuse to acknowledge God at all, and think that we are self sufficient without Him. We then can develop an arrogant attitude that says, "I did it all and I am a self made man."

One of the weaknesses of human nature is that when we discover a truth, we have a tendency to focus on it to the extent that we ignore other truths. We can go from being in the ditch on one side of the road and then swing right over into the ditch on the other side of the road, rather than being properly balanced in the middle. Those who are well grounded in both practical self help materials and also rooted in spiritual truths concerning the necessity for God's help throughout life will have a healthy life balance. They will have discovered **the secret combination** that will open the lock to all the good that this abundant life has to offer.

SUMMARY

Abraham, Isaac, Jacob, Joseph, Moses and Jesus were not only prosperity teachers, but also millionaires themselves.

Everything in the kingdom works by faith, and nothing in the kingdom works without faith. All things are possible, for them that believe.

It is the faith and expectation of God keeping His word, and doing what He said He would do, that brings into manifestation that which has been promised.

The nearer we live to the source of wealth, the more wealth we shall receive.

There is a power and when it is activated in your life, it will be as though you are being assisted by unseen forces, and indeed you are.

Activating spiritual assistance by faith can accelerate your progress far beyond your natural ability would be able to achieve in the same period of time.

A miracle can get you out of immediate trouble, but ignorance will simply recreate your crisis.

We have our part to play and God has His part to play. We cannot do God's part for Him and He will not do our part for us.

The secret combination will open the lock to all the good that this abundant life has to offer.

Chapter 7

How to Use Affirmations to Change Your World

How Our Spirit Shapes Our Future

Everything that is showing up in our experience *externally* is an exact reflection of what is going on in our world *internally*. When you get the inside right, the outside will begin to align itself with it. Some psychologists believe that lasting success is made up of 98% mental preparation, and 2% outward action. New Year's resolutions usually don't last very long, simply because the new direction has not been successfully passed on from the conscious mind to the subconscious mind as a *definite* command. When a desire has been firmly planted in your spirit, come hell or high water, *nothing* will be able to stop you from achieving it. When you have conceived it on the inside, it will begin to show up on the outside, guaranteed.

"Whatever we plant in our subconscious mind and nourish with repetition and emotion will one day become a reality."

—Earl Nightingale—

Our spirit shapes our future, whether it's an individual, a team, a company or an entire nation. Things can get much better, they can get much worse or they can pretty much remain the same. The great motivational speaker Jim Rohn used to say, "The only way it gets better for you is when *you* get better." Better is not something that you wish for, it is something you become. You can change *all things* for the better when you change yourself for the better. This realisation is the reason why self help and personal development has become so popular. **The greatest investment you can make is to invest in yourself. The only way your life will change, is if you do.**

Often our attempts to improve are short lived. Whether it is to get ahead financially, or to diet and exercise until we achieve our ideal weight and fitness. Sadly and frustratingly even if we do reach a particular goal, it's not long before we slip back into our old ways and end up right back where we started. Most of our attempts to diet do not achieve long lasting results, because our internal set point which is made up of our self concept, our self image and our self esteem brings us right back to whatever we believe deep down that we are. You will never outperform the person that you *think* you are.

Your self—image is the way you *see* yourself. Your self-esteem is the way you *feel* about yourself. So your self-concept is basically the way you think, see and feel about yourself. Your self—concept determines the way you act, and your actions determine your results.

BY THEIR FRUITS YOU SHALL KNOW THEM

The ancient text in several places likens individuals to trees. Jesus said, "By their *fruits* you shall know *them*." The fruits on the outside reveal what is truly on the inside. If for example the fruits are small, hard and taste bitter, that would indicate that *we* on the inside are small minded and throughout life *we* have become hardened and bitter. The outer world is the world of effects and the inner world is the world of causes. Louise L. Hay advises that, "Continuous modes of thinking and speaking produce body behaviours and postures and "eases," or diseases. **The person who has a permanently scowling face didn't produce that by having joyous, loving thoughts**." Human beings have far more power and authority over all the effects in their lives than most of us realise.

"If you want to change the fruits, you will first have to change the roots.

If you want to change the visible, you must first change the invisible."

—T Harv Eker—

Your current inner beliefs have been formed within you over years of affirming and reaffirming those convictions. Even if they are totally untrue, if you believe them you will produce effects in alignment with them. Our past programming or conditioning is the root cause of the fruits that are repeatedly showing up in our lives. Whether it's in the form of our physical health, our relationships, or in our finances, unless we identify our subconscious programming and change it for the better, it will continue to produce the same kind of results for the rest of our lives.

AFFIRM YOUR WAY TO A MORE PROSPEROUS LIFE

Many of our convictions have been formed by *words* that we have heard others say about us and also by words spoken about life in general, sayings that have been passed around sometimes for generations that we have heard repeatedly and have accepted as being true. Understanding the huge significance that our mental programming has on every area of our lives, we must begin to deliberately choose, challenge and change our thinking so that it supports us and empowers us to bear fruits of success and well being on every branch of our tree. The words that others have spoken about you do not have the same level of impact on you as the words that *you* have spoken about yourself. Make your words work *for* you, not against you. The answer to most of our problems is right under our nose, literally. **You can turn your life around by the power of your tongue.**

Whenever you affirm a thing, you are making it firm in your life. Think honestly about the following questions. Are you regularly affirming how awesome life is, or how awful life is? What do you say when you talk to yourself? What are the regular grove tracks of your internal dialogue? Are you building yourself up or putting yourself down? What are your regular sayings on the subject of money?

> "The only way to permanently change the temperature in the room is to reset the thermostat.
>
> In the same way, the only way to change your level of financial success permanently is to reset your financial thermostat."
>
> —T. Harv Eker—

When you become friendly towards prosperity by the way you think and speak about it, prosperity will become friendly towards you. If you are antagonistic towards prosperity and talk about it as though it is an enemy, don't expect to have an abundance of it in your life. But the moment you change your attitude towards it and this change is expressed through your thoughts and words, prosperity will *immediately* begin to be attracted to you.

> "There is nothing wrong with wanting to get rich. The desire for riches is really the desire for a richer, fuller, and more abundant life; And that desire is praiseworthy."
> —Wallace D Wattles—

When you affirm this statement to yourself, if there is a conflicting belief within you that resists it, that resistance is evidence that your current subconscious programming is set to *resist* wealth. **The only way to reset this internal programme is by deliberately writing a new programme through the power of affirmations.** Affirmations should be present tense, personal and passionate.

The following lists of affirmations can help you to reprogram your mind for total life success. It's a true principle that **whatever you repeatedly hear, you will eventually believe**. I recommend reading aloud each individual affirmation at least three times for deeper mind acceptance.

> "Any thought that is passed onto the subconscious often enough and convincingly enough is finally accepted."
> —Robert Collier—

AFFIRMATIONS CONCERNING THE POWER OF YOUR WORDS

My words are seeds that produce an abundant harvest according to their kind.

As I change my thoughts and words, my world around me begins to change.

My words are charged with prospering power.

What I say is what I get.

I decree a thing and it is established for me.

Death and life are in the power of the tongue.

Whoever shall say and shall not doubt in his heart, but shall believe that those things which he says shall come to pass, he shall have whatever he says.

I speak the word and it comes to pass.

My words are filled with creative power.

I choose to think and speak in ways that will support and empower me toward success and happiness, instead of in ways that don't.

AFFIRMATIONS FOR LIFE SUCCESS

I am happy, I am healthy and I feel terrific.

I am thankful and grateful for all the good in my life.

It's a wonderful life.

Whatever my mind can conceive and believe, I can achieve.

I can do it.

I radiate success, and I attract success.

I am open and receptive to all the good, and all the abundance that life has to offer.

I am mastering the art of receiving.

The floodgates of heaven are open over my life, and I am blessed to be a blessing.

I am supernaturally protected and directed, preserved and prospered by the ministry of angels.

No evil shall befall me, nor shall any calamity come near my dwelling, for He will command His angels concerning me to guard me in all my ways.

I am continually increasing the quality and the quantity of my contribution, and I am continually receiving an increase in quality and quantity of rewards.

I am meant to have an amazing life.

I vividly visualise myself as the person I desire to be.

I can be, do and have anything I truly put my mind to.

I am creative and resourceful and have all the abilities I need to succeed.

It's fun and easy to take action toward my goals.

I am deeply grateful for the freedom I have to move and act toward my goals.

I programme my mind for success.

I think positive thoughts, I send out positive vibes and I attract back positive things.

I consciously observe my thoughts and entertain only those that will empower me.

Every day in every way, I am getting better and better.

I like myself, I respect myself and I like being me.

It's great to be alive.

I express myself freely.

Every day is a new and exciting adventure.

Life is good. Life is so good.

Lots can happen in a relatively short period of time.

I am worthy of receiving all the good that I desire.

I have a success filled spiritual aura all around me that attracts into my life wonderful things every day.

AFFIRMATIONS FOR HEALTH AND VITALITY

I am alive and well, and every fibre of my being radiates life and health.

Every day I receive fresh life and vitality, and I am grateful.

Every cell of my body is filled with divine energy, and I am alive with the life of God.

No sickness or disease will rule over me. I exercise my God given power and authority.

Every fibre of my being is saturated with life and health.

From the top of my head to the soles of my feet, I am healthy and well all the days of my life.

I appreciate my health.

Every joint in my body functions in the perfection that God created them to function in, all the days of my life.

No evil shall befall me, nor shall any plague come near my dwelling.

I am happy, I am healthy, I am blessed, I am anointed and I am filled with the power of God.

AFFIRMATIONS FOR WEALTH AND PROSPERITY

Wisdom and wealth are flowing to me and through me every day of my life.

Whatever I put my hands to shall prosper.

I am a money magnet.

Money comes to me in avalanches of abundance.

Every blockage to my prosperity is being divinely dissolved now. Abundant increase is flowing freely to me. All resistance is taken out of the way.

Money comes to me in ever increasing quantities from multiple sources on a continuous basis.

There is always more than enough.

Wealth and riches are in my house.

I open my mind to prosperity.

I practice prosperous thinking.

My prosperous thinking produces prosperous results.

I welcome money like a good friend, because it is.

I speak supernatural increase upon my financial net worth.

All my financial investments are divinely protected and divinely prospered.

I remember the Lord my God, for it is He who gives me power to get wealth.

I appreciate my financial prosperity.

I am definite about prosperity and prosperity is definite about me.

Money is circulating freely in my life. It flows to me in avalanches of abundance.

Money is attracted to me, money is my friend.

I've decided to open my mind to receive prosperity on a higher level than ever before.

Wealth is pouring into my life.

I experience a continuous flow of prosperity

Money comes to me easily, for I am a money magnet.

I live in a world of abundance.

Prosperity is attracted to me and I am attracted to prosperity.

Money likes me, because I appreciate it and respect it.

I radiate wealth and success vibes.

I magnetise wealth and riches.

I am helping others to become more prosperous and I am becoming more prosperous myself in the process.

My mind is set for financial liberty.

I open my mind to receive life's lavish abundance.

I open my heart and I open my spirit to receive wealth and riches on a higher level than ever before.

I have made a commitment to attract abundant life.

Thank you.

SUMMARY

When you get the inside right, the outside will begin to align itself with it.

When a desire has been firmly planted in your spirit, nothing will be able to stop you from achieving it.

Our spirit shapes our future.

You can change *all things* for the better when you change yourself for the better.

You will never outperform the person you *think* you are.

Our past programming or conditioning is the root cause of the fruits that are repeatedly showing up in our lives.

Human beings have far more power and authority over all the effects in their lives than most of us realise.

Any thought that is passed onto the subconscious often enough and convincingly enough is finally accepted

When you become friendly towards prosperity by the way you think and speak about it, prosperity will become friendly towards you.

You can turn your life around by the power of your tongue.